Warp Speed Habits

Warp Speed Habits

A Brain-Based Roadmap for Leveraging Change in Organizations

Marco Neves

BEP

BUSINESS EXPERT PRESS

Leader in applied, concise business books

Warp Speed Habits:
A Brain-Based Roadmap for Leveraging Change in Organizations

Copyright © Marco Neves, 2024

Cover design by Marco Neves

Interior design by Exeter Premedia Services Private Ltd., Chennai, India

First published in 2023 by
Business Expert Press, LLC
222 East 46th Street, New York, NY 10017
www.businessexpertpress.com

ISBN-13: 978-1-63742-506-0 (paperback)
ISBN-13: 978-1-63742-507-7 (e-book)

Business Expert Press Human Resource Management and Organizational Behavior Collection

First edition: 2023

10 9 8 7 6 5 4 3 2 1

To Ana, my life partner, and to my daughters Inês and Mariana,
you are my True North and Guiding Lights.

Description

What if you could adapt rapidly to change, design your destiny, plot your own North, systematically design the roads you wish to travel, and go the distance–improving your health, your work, and your life?

Change means that you will have to create habits, and as both individuals and organizations have found, this is **an extremely challenging venture**. You may feel that procedures and methods, allied with inspiration, willpower, and motivation, will be enough, but the up and down nature of the latter qualities can lead to repeated failed attempts.

For individuals, leaders, managers, or anyone who wishes to build or change habits and behaviors and acquire new competencies, **the answer lies in** *Warp Speed Habits*, a **revolutionary brain-based strategic–tactical approach** to creating habits and changing behaviors.

Intersecting **neuroscience and psychology**, this guide **leverages business management lessons at an individual level**, promotes the **development of a "habit mindset,"** and **reshapes environmental contexts**. In this quest, as you learn to design, build, and implement sustainable habits, you will **travel to worlds and dimensions in different realms**.

Ready? Begin your first voyage, but make no mistake, as you execute missions in your voyages, do not illude yourself by biographies of overnight success—these are myths that blur the mindset of energy and resilience you will require.

But with the *Warp Speed Habits* **practical and pragmatical roadmap**, you will overcome brain traps and obstacles along the way, and ultimately **contribute to thriving behaviors that deliver results!**

Keywords

habits; science of habits; strategy and tactics; business transformation; organizational change; culture change; learning organization; behavior change

Contents

Testimonials xi

Preface xiii

Acknowledgments.. xv

Warp Speed Habits Primer xvii

The Habits Challenge xix

Your Quest xxi

Part 1   **The Novice**... 1
Voyage I   Brain Science, Business Thinking, Habits Mindset,
              and Environmental Contexts...3

Part 2   **The Scientist** 19
Voyage II   From the Amazon Rainforest to Europe 21
Voyage III   Friends or Foes 37
Voyage IV   Identity System—Illusions and Mindsets 49

Part 3   **The Painter** 57
Voyage V   Strategy and Tactics...59
Voyage VI   The Habits Strategic Canvas.......................................65

Part 4   **The Maestro/a**.. 97
Voyage VII   The Strategy–Tactic Intersection 99
Voyage VIII   The Habits Tactical Sheet...113
Voyage IX   Full Cycle—From Tactics to Strategy........................153

Part 5   **The Architect** 159
Voyage X   Taking Habits to the Next Level................................161

Part 6   **The Learner**.. 175
Voyage XI   Move Your Vision and Goals Closer 177

Create Your Habits at Warp Speed 183
Appendixes 185
Appendix I: Michael's Action-Responses 187
Appendix II: A Description of Michael's Measures 191
Appendix III: Daily DOSE Activities 193
References 195
About the Author 205
Index 207

Testimonials

"Warp Speed Habits *brings us a disruptive view on how we make things happen consistently in Management. What is the purpose of wanting to move forward, if we don't master and understand what is behind our will? Marco has put order on what we thought was random and brings us a roadmap to learn and develop habits of success in our daily tasks.*

This book highlights the importance of linking Management and Neuroscience; it is definitely a 'one step ahead' framework." —**Bruno Silva, Executive Board Member, Group Trofa Saúde**

"Warp Speed Habits *is a must-read book for all, for our professional and personal growth. The journey provided by Marco, in this excellent knowledge tool, boosts and drives the transformation required in these turbulent times, linking strategy with tactics, through 'habits' in a very innovative way."* —**Amâncio Torres, Middle East Managing Partner, SIA PARTNERS**

"Warp Speed Habits *presents us with an innovative and structured approach to the journey of understanding and mastering something so important to our personal and professional lives as our day-to-day habits. 'We first make our habits and then our habits make us' … a very simple but compelling truth.*

The way Marco proposes us to undertake this step-by-step journey is very creative. With a sound scientific background but also pragmatic hints, the avatars evolve through progressive challenges and deeper insights into the voyage of knowing and challenging ourselves and connecting our daily behaviors with our team's performance and our organization's strategies.

Without a doubt a very useful model for anyone who wants to challenge and master their habits." —**João Pacheco De Castro, Senior Partner, Eurogroup Consulting, Lisbon**

"Warp Speed Habits *connects Management, Leadership and Neuroscience in a pragmatic book, driving us to think and act.*

In a metaphorical manner, accompanied by practical activities and exercises, this model addresses how behaviors and habits can help us evolve individually or as part of a team, in the same way that they can limit our process of continuous improvement.

Ultimately a journey that, through the personification of six avatars carrying out diverse missions, we can tangibilize in our daily lives."
—**Paula Arriscado (PhD), Corporate Division Director, People, Brand and Communication, Group Salvador Caetano**

"*In an increasingly volatile and complex world, the search for great performance is increasingly a fundamental objective for leaders.*

This performance is directly related to the ability of organizations to change, which, in turn, depends on the ability of people to transform themselves.

To achieve this, Warp Speed Habits *proposes a strategic-tactical quest with the positive contribution of neuroscience, allowing for a faster assessment of the evolution of people and organizations. And in this manner, the structuring of a journey that allows us to accelerate our evolution."* —**Pierre Debourdeau, Managing Partner, Eurogroup Consulting, Lisbon**

Preface

For over three decades, I have had the fortune of working in the fields of strategy definition, reengineering, organizational change, and leadership development.

In 2016, I came across an article covering the importance of neuroscience to organizations. I found it both fascinating and practical. Insights and scientific evidence to leverage behavioral change were coming to the fore.

Over the last six years, I've drawn on and combined these insights with strategy, business management, and psychology, among others, to create *Warp Speed Habits*.

Various leadership development initiatives have also helped to enhance this model, culminating in this book, *Warp Speed Habits: A Brain-Based Roadmap for Leveraging Change in Organizations*.

By using the step-by-step strategic–tactical approach and solutions described in this book, you can practice creating habits on a daily basis, taking on challenges, and overcoming mental blocks.

Through the brain-based *Warp Speed Habits* approach, you will power your habits and unlock your potential to achieve optimal levels of performance!

Acknowledgments

It has been a privilege to have worked with and learned from the research of neuroscientists, psychologists, business leaders, subject matter experts, and authors.

The input of my clients and partners across EMEA where we have explored and implemented these approaches has also been instrumental.

Their feedback underlines the need to leverage science in behavioral change and reinforces my belief that neuroscience makes a beneficial difference across organizations.

It was with appreciation that I also received fundamental input from the readers of the first version of this book. A special thanks to Bruno Silva for his global oversight, Amâncio Torres for his strategic perspective, Pierre Debourdeau and João Castro for their structured and critical feedback, and Paula Arriscado for her insightful perspectives.

I am grateful to the team at Business Expert Press for their enthusiasm, charm, and timeliness in their feedback. Thank you to Scott Isenberg and Michael Provitera for their structured input and Charlene Kronstedt for her marketing and production support. Also, thanks to Exeter team for their patience and a fantastic job in the book's interior design.

I also owe thanks to hundreds of people I have worked with within my professional career. Together, our journeys have allowed me to build an integrated approach that is a fundamental basis for leveraging individual change in organizations.

Most of all, I thank my family for their unlimited understanding and love. This book is dedicated to them.

Finally, this is a living, breathing framework. It must be, considering the world we live in. As I continue to work with organizations, partners, and individuals, I look forward to, together, honing this approach with further insights and solutions.

Warp Speed Habits Primer

Warp Speed Habits *plural noun*

Definition of Habits

- Psychology: An automatic behavior that is carried out with little guidance, intention, or deliberate thought, in response to a specific situation.
- Neuroscience: A motor or cognitive routine that is triggered by the brain in response to stimuli and completed with unconscious competence.

Definition of Warp Speed

- An extremely high speed.
- Origin: from the popular 1970s' U.S. television series Star Trek.
- Originally referring to a faster-than-light speed attained by Starship Enterprise traveling in a space warp, exploring the Final Frontier of Space, carrying its crew on missions to discover strange, new worlds; to seek new life and new civilizations; to boldly go where no man has gone before.

Definition of Warp Speed Habits

A consolidated approach to design, build, and implement organizational habits to change behaviors and cultures.

Attained by taking your people on missions to explore the *Final Frontier* of the brain; to leverage the business management strategic and tactical logic required to create habits; and to purposefully promote mindsets and shape environments that facilitate the creation of habits across the organization.

The Habits Challenge

Frederick Herzberg, one of the most influential names in business management, asserted that the most captivating growth forces in life are achievements and being recognized for achievements, challenges and the opportunities to learn, and contributing to others, enlightening our paths as we grow [1].

In the same vein, Carol Dweck examines the mindsets people use to structure the "self" and guide their behavior. She illuminates how the power of believing that we can improve—a growth mindset—can propel us to fulfill our potential. With this frame of mind, individuals embrace challenges, persist in the face of setbacks, see effort as the path to mastery, learn from criticism, and find inspiration in the success of others [2].

Perhaps powerful phrases like these, or when you are searching for meaning at work, or take part in organizationwide strategy, leadership, or change programs, or even from feelings of emotional discomfort, are the ones that motivate you to take a step forward. In these situations, you are encouraged to become more mindful and contemplative and feel empowered to grow your mindset and enhance different aspects of your "self."

At some point in your life, given similar circumstances, you will have attempted to create habits to change your behaviors. You thought it would be easy. You wanted to change and were motivated. You found, however, that building habits was difficult, and you were unsuccessful in most of your attempts.

You may think that inspiration, willpower, and motivation are enough. The variable nature of these qualities, however, can lead to repeated failed attempts. Not understanding this, you may even have felt ashamed of your lack of progress.

Don't berate yourself. Time pressure, fluctuations in willpower and motivation, distractions, and even hunger leads to failure in attempts at building habits. This is a problem that has long confounded humanity.

So, how can you build habits consciously and consistently, as opposed to these growing inadvertently?

The answer lies in your *Warp Speed Habits* quest.

You will travel from the inner depths of your brain to the business logic that companies use in defining their strategies, and then onto other realms further afield. These are the places where you will find the ingredients to create habits.

You will apply these to your situation, make the learning your own, experiment as you go, and increase your chances of success to leverage change at an individual, team, and organizational level.

Your Quest

Watch your thoughts, they become your words; watch your words, they become your actions; watch your actions, they become your habits; watch your habits, they become your character; watch your character, it becomes your destiny.

—Lao Tzu

Just like the captain and crew of *Starship Enterprise* in *Star Trek*, in their voyages and missions to discover new worlds, and a submarine crew in *Fantastic Voyage*, reduced to microscopic size to repair damage to a scientist's brain, in *Warp Speed Habits*, you will travel to and explore different worlds in your quest to create and change habits.

In these voyages, you will execute various missions as you explore new ways of building habits and changing behaviors in organizations.

You will venture into the *Final Frontier*[1], your brain, central to human behavior, where there is still far more unknown and unchartered territory than known.

You will deploy business management logic, learn to apply strategy at a personal level, and intersect and integrate this dimension with your tactics.

You will also learn to promote a habits mindset through a holistic framework and shape your environment to incorporate physical, social, and emotional perspectives that are fundamental to the creation of habits.

---

[1] Inspired by *Star Trek* and by *Fantastic Voyage*: the former, by creating a sense of awe, much as when it comes to exploring the *Final Frontier* of the brain; the latter, by stretching our imagination in the 1966 American science fiction story by Otto Klement and Jerome Bixby, about a submarine crew who are shrunk to microscopic size and venture into the body of an injured scientist to repair damage to his brain.

During your quest, you will take on the role of six avatars (see Figure Y.1), as you beam across to different dimensions, engage in 11 voyages (see Figure Y.2), and complete 48 missions in sequential order.

The
Novice

The
Scientist

The
Painter

The
Maestro/a

The
Architect

The
Learner

Figure Y.1 Your avatars

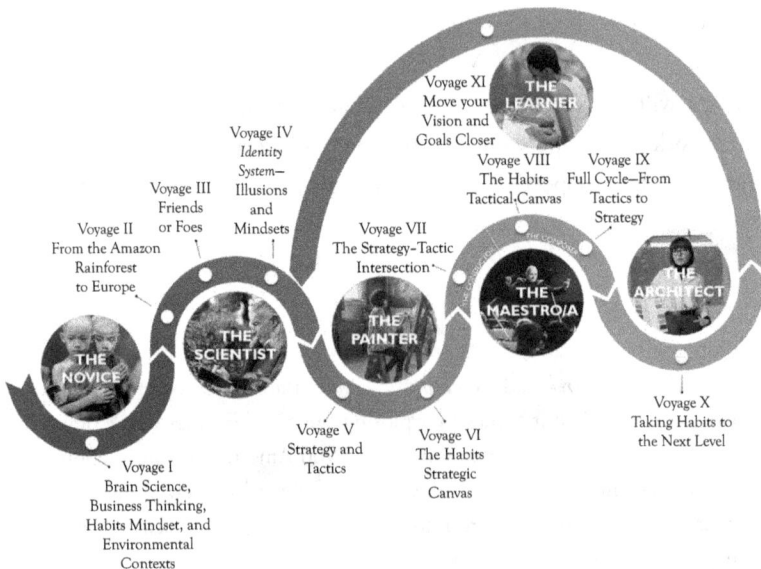

Voyage XI
Move your
Vision and
Goals Closer

THE
LEARNER

Voyage IV
*Identity
System—*
Illusions
and
Mindsets

Voyage III
Friends
or Foes

Voyage VIII
The Habits
Tactical Canvas

Voyage IX
Full Cycle—From
Tactics to
Strategy

Voyage II
From the Amazon
Rainforest
to Europe

Voyage VII
The Strategy-Tactic
Intersection

THE
SCIENTIST

THE
PAINTER

THE
MAESTRO/A

THE
ARCHITECT

THE
NOVICE

Voyage X
Taking Habits to
the Next Level

Voyage I
Brain Science,
Business Thinking,
Habits Mindset, and
Environmental
Contexts

Voyage V
Strategy and
Tactics

Voyage VI
The Habits
Strategic
Canvas

Figure Y.2 Your voyages

You will understand the realm of each destination you visit, as you log your experiences in your *Warp Speed Habits Workbook*[2]. I encourage you to use this workbook in your travels—this will help you in your learning process.

These are your voyages and avatars:

- In **Voyage I**, you are a **novice**, an individual who is unacquainted or unskilled in the science and art of building habits, as you execute missions to understand that habits are a part of your life. You will grasp that you need to intersect neuroscience and psychology, apply business thinking, promote a habits mindset, and shape environmental contexts.

- In your **second to fourth voyages**, you will be a **scientist**, a person who will gain a system of scientific knowledge covering the general laws of what makes the brain tick when building or changing habits. You can be Madame Curie or Albert Einstein, revered for their scientific accomplishments, as you roam through the *Final Frontier*.

  In your **second voyage**, you will travel from the Amazon rainforest to southern Europe in a microscopic turbine-engine vessel, understand your brain's complexity and the enormous potential you have to learn and grow.

  In **Voyage III**, you will travel to different brain systems[3]. You will uncover the basic machinery behind habits, comprehend why you resist change, and the conditions necessary to build habits.

  In your **fourth voyage**, back at your desk, you will review the information acquired. You will reflect on the illusion and mindset of your *Identity System*[4] and what is required to rebuild and enhance it.

---

[2] Download your workbook from www.warpspeedhabits.com

[3] Joseph LeDoux, a professor of neuroscience and psychology at New York University, states that you need to think of your behaviors as products of systems rather than of specific areas in the brain. Neurons in specific areas are part of and contribute to a global system.

[4] The term *Identity System* is used in this book to capture the essence of your core values, beliefs, mindsets, and preferences.

- Armed with this knowledge, in **Voyages V and VI**, you will take on one of your more fundamental roles as a **painter**, an artist who will paint self-portraits, both of current and desired states of identities, behaviors, and habits. You can be the Pablo Picasso or Frida Kahlo of painting habits, two of the most influential artists of the 20th century.

  During your **fifth voyage**, you will understand the strategic underpinnings required for change, and in **Voyage VI**, you will use the *Habits Strategic Canvas*, a component of the strategic–tactical framework, to paint your behavioral autobiography and future self. This is a fundamental base to build habits.

  From the **seventh to ninth voyages**, you will take on another foundational role as a **maestro or maestra**, an eminent composer and conductor, as you coordinate a powerful *Habits Quartet*[5] and compose a repertoire of *Habits Scores*[6] for your habits using the *Habits Tactical Sheet*. You can be Sir Simon Rattle or Marin Alsop, two of the world's greatest conductors, as you achieve the required consistency to build habits.

- During the **10th Voyage**, you will be an **architect**, a designer of the broad social, emotional, and physical organizational contexts at the points of choice, as you reduce or amplify decisions to facilitate the creation of habits.
  You can choose to be Antoni Gaudí or Jeanne Gang, two of the most prominent architects of their generations, as you design and implement social, emotional, and physical environments that will be conducive to building effective habits.

- In your **11th and final voyage**, as a **learner**, you will be yourself. Recapping your lessons and solutions, you will use visualization techniques to practice executing your process and achieving your future goals.

---

[5] Refers to the four components of habits, covered in depth in the seventh voyage.

[6] Written composition describing how the habits components "play" together.

Throughout your voyages, you will take on board lessons from Michael. He will be your buddy during this journey, someone who will share his outputs from his strategic and tactical missions with you, as he works toward achieving his quest.

One last note. This quest is about you and your avatars, and the hero or heroine you will be as you complete your missions during your voyages.

With this integrated approach to building and changing habits, you can deliberately take on rewarding challenges to achieve the performances of your life.

I wish you a successful quest!

PART 1

The Novice

An individual who is unacquainted or unskilled in the science and art of building habits.

Your quest has begun, and you assume your first avatar, the novice, as you prepare to launch yourself into your maiden voyage, *Brain Science, Business Thinking, Habits Mindset, and Environmental Contexts.*

You are a newcomer and a learner during this exploratory voyage, as you begin to understand that habits are a part of your identity. Despite your best intentions to create and change habits, you will understand that you probably are not effective at building habits, and these seem to keep you on the same path in your everyday life (see Figure 1.1).

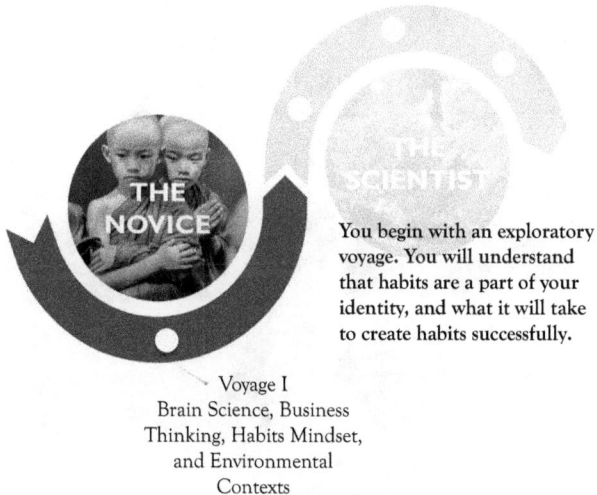

You begin with an exploratory voyage. You will understand that habits are a part of your identity, and what it will take to create habits successfully.

Voyage I
Brain Science, Business
Thinking, Habits Mindset,
and Environmental
Contexts

Figure 1.1 Your maiden voyage

Before you begin, a final note. Do not illude yourself by biographies of overnight success—these are myths that blur the mindset of energy and self-discipline you will require.

In your travels to different worlds, your resilience in executing missions and overcoming obstacles in different realms is fundamental—this isn't a quick fix; it takes time and sustained effort.

Ready? Let's begin your first voyage!

VOYAGE I

Brain Science, Business Thinking, Habits Mindset, and Environmental Contexts

Habits seem to keep you doing what you've always done, despite your best intentions to change.

As the novice, the **objectives for your first voyage** are:

⊕ Understand **how effective you currently are in creating habits**.

⊕ Understand **what it will take to create habits** successfully.

***

To achieve these objectives, you will need to execute the following six missions:

🚀 Mission 1: The Habits Quartet
🚀 Mission 2: Are You Effective at Building Habits?
🚀 Mission 3: Are You in Control?
🚀 Mission 4: Reflecting Upon Strategy and Tactics
🚀 Mission 5: Do You Have a "Habits Growth Mindset"?
🚀 Mission 6: Does Your Environment Affect Your Habits?

***

If you are asked what the word "habit" means, you will probably reply along the lines of: "A habit is a repeated and automatic behavior or action, including feeling, thinking, or doing."

The next question could be, "What leads to a behavior becoming regular and automatic?" You would probably have to give this question some thought before replying.

Habits Defined

Research shows that **a habit is a behavior that we carry out in response to triggers**. These are linked to stable contexts—persons, locations, preceding actions, emotions, and events—in our environment [3, 4].

After a certain amount of repetition, we display the **same default mode of response or behavioral pattern that persists with little guidance, intention, or deliberate thought** [5, 6].

We can break this definition of a habit down into four components,[1] shown in bold in the example here:

1. You arrive at work each morning and a to-do list will be the first item you see—the to-do list is the **trigger**.
2. This is the cue that prompts you into an **action-response**. The to-do list trigger will "push" you to review your outstanding to-dos and include new items with allocated time slots.
3. You will feel satisfaction when you prioritize your work. This **reward** is dopamine released by your brain, leading to a cycle of motivation and reinforcement.
4. When you sit down at your desk first thing in the morning, you will unconsciously anticipate the sense of satisfaction from updating your to-do list. This is **craving** in the form of dopamine being released as you anticipate your reward.

During the day, you will continue to be **triggered** by your to-do list to execute an **action-response** (review and update your to-dos), giving you a **rewarding** sense of satisfied accomplishment.

---

[1] The concept of these stages, discovered by MIT researchers in the 1990s, is the core of every habit and is based on a simple neurological loop. This concept was popularized by Charles Duhigg with "The Habit Loop" (Cue–Routine–Reward) and "The Craving Brain" in his book *The Power of Habit* and by James Clear with the four-step pattern (Cue–Craving–Response–Reward) in his book *Atomic Habits*.

The **reward** helps your brain understand that this behavior is important to remember. It does this by creating **cravings** that eventually lead to a habit being formed.

From the example earlier, you can see that the triggers will only be effective when you establish a connection between the trigger (to-do list) and the anticipation or craving (dopamine hits) of the reward (more dopamine hits).

***

🚀 Mission 1: The Habits Quartet

Think about your working day and your current habits.

Now, based on the four components shown in the to-do list example earlier, complete Table I.1 in your workbook with two to three examples of your current habits.

Table I.1 Examples of your current habits

Trigger	Action-response	Reward	Craving

Were you able to identify each of the four components of your current habits?

If not, do not be concerned. We will cover these in more detail when you assume your maestro or maestra avatar.

***

A Fundamental Basis for Many of Your Daily Actions

You move through life believing you are an informed, rational, and conscious decision maker.

Neuroscience, however, shows that many of the decisions and choices you make every day are based on your implicit memory,[2] where your habits are stored.

---

[2] Sometimes referred to as unconscious or automatic memory. Implicit memory uses experiences to remember things without thinking about them.

Curiously, although our perception is that we control our daily activities, up to half of these are based on habits rather than choices (see Table I.2).

Table I.2 *Habitual daily behaviors*

Almost **50 percent** of behaviors are performed without thoughts about these [7].
About **40 percent** of **daily activities** occur each day **in almost the same situations** [8].
About **45 percent** of **behaviors** occur in the **same physical location** almost every day [7].

This pervasive effect of habits in everyday behavior results from **decades of mental programming by your brain.** You learned these ingrained routines in your childhood and early adulthood, from your parents, your teachers, your peer groups, or **influenced by diverse social and emotional environmental contexts.**

These routines, grounded in your unique experiences, have **contributed to the basis of your core values, beliefs, mindsets, and preferences, your** *Identity System*, where, once habits take root, they persist with little deliberation or reconsideration.

Regardless of how habits govern your behavior, because they occur outside your spectrum of thoughts, guided by context, and performed without conscious thought, you are incapable of knowing how prevalent and influential they are.

While habits, the fundamental basis for many of your daily actions, help you operate efficiently, you perform these rigidly. Habits are powerful barriers to behavioral change, setting limits and interfering with your intentions, attitudes, and decisions to change.

Complex electrochemical reactions play out every second in the grooved mass that is your brain, much of it unconsciously, easily pulling you back into old and existing routines.

Your brain "makes you forget" new habits, overriding knowledge and intentions to act, tipping the balance, and slipping you back into old routines that you've practiced your entire life. Habits seem to keep you doing what you've always done, despite your best intentions to change.

But it is these habits, reliant on automatic processes, that tell you and the world around you who you are.

Decisions that you make today, actions and decisions you once took, now solidified in strong habits, form the wide foundation of your behaviors.

These will continue to mold your behavior, determining to a large degree how you act and how this affects the creation and functioning of organizational cultures!

Your next mission will give you a glimpse of why this happens (remember to use your *Warp Speed Habits Workbook* to document your findings).[3]

***

🚀 Mission 2: Are You Effective at Building Habits?

Answer the following Yes/No questions to understand your ability to build habits:

- I understand what it takes to create or change habits?
- I use a specific method to create and/or change habits?
- I link the habits I want to create or change with my "why," my vision of my future?
- Most of the time, I'm successful when I attempt to create a habit?
- I recognize that peer groups may positively or negatively affect the creation of habits and have put in place solutions to leverage or minimize this effect?
- When I am unsuccessful in creating or changing habits, I do not put it down to a lack of time, willpower, or motivation?

Not answering positively to some of these questions shows an opportunity you have to master the art and science of building habits.

***

---

[3] You will find this first mission easy to execute. As you complete your voyages, the complexity of your successive missions will vary in intensity.

To become successful in creating habits, you will need to embrace and **apply practical insights from the intersection of neuroscience and psychology**, **onboard business management lessons**, **develop a habits mindset**, and **shape your environment** to create new habits or change old ones.

A Dialogue: Psychology and Neuroscience

Your brain should need no introduction. After all, it is your brain that makes you "you!"

It is, however, a paradox that the organ that helps you understand and guides your interaction with your world needs to be better comprehended.

Thanks to technological advances and stunning neuroscience research,[4] scientific evidence and insights are beginning to reveal the complex universe in your head.

Born from the question "How do our brains work?" the focus of the application of neuroscience has been mainly in the health sector, in the diagnosis and treatment of neurological and psychiatric diseases. With increasing contributions to advertising, marketing, military, education, and other sectors, methods and tools have also been leveraged to enhance the performance of leaders, teams, and organizations.

Though neuroscience research into creating habits and long-term behavior change has only emerged over the last few decades, it has become instrumental in advancing the scientific comprehension of habit creation.

It is at this intersection of neuroscience and psychology that breakthroughs have occurred. The study of the anatomy and physiology of the brain, including molecular and cellular studies of individual neurons, and images of sensory, motor, and cognitive tasks, overlapping the study of the mind and human nature, including our deepest thoughts, feelings, assumptions, beliefs, and behaviors, have revealed important insights.

---

[4] The science that studies the anatomy and physiology of the nervous system.

Based on brain-level insights and explanations focusing on habits and behavioral change within organizational contexts in areas of cognition, learning, and behavior, you will be able to:

- Understand **how habits work** and **how creating habits can go wrong**.
- Understand that beyond the brain's automaticity is **your mind and consciousness that will allow you to define your future habits** as you **"become aware of being aware."**
- Implement **a systemic brain approach that will allow you to create habits in a consistent and deliberate manner**, mitigating difficulties and increasing your success in this quest.

***

🚀 Mission 3: Are You in Control?

Is it possible that part of your brain "wills" an action before you are consciously aware of it? Perform the following experiment to find out (see Figure I.1):

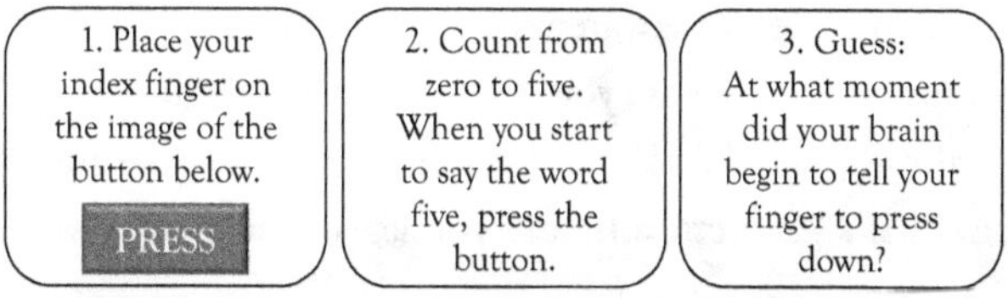

1. Place your index finger on the image of the button below. PRESS	2. Count from zero to five. When you start to say the word five, press the button.	3. Guess: At what moment did your brain begin to tell your finger to press down?

Figure I.1 Are you in control?

***

In the 1960s, two German researchers, Hans Helmut Kornhuber and Luder Deecke, used electroencephalogram (EEG) devices to measure the brain's electrical sensitivity of test subjects executing simple finger movements [9].

When the EEG results were compared with electromyograph recordings (that evaluate the response of muscle movements against nerve stimulation), a precursor spike was detected in the brain 1.5 seconds before the muscle movement! This was called readiness potential.

In the early 1980s, the late neuroscientist, Benjamin Libet, added an element to this research [10]. In a series of experiments, volunteers used a clock to pinpoint the instant their conscious awareness "wanted" to perform a simple task such as pressing a button or flexing their wrist.

These experiments consistently showed that there was unconscious brain activity (a change in EEG signals) associated with the action for an average of three-tenths of a second before the participants' (subjective) awareness of their decision to move.

In a more recent study [11], the brain activity of volunteers was measured using functional magnetic resonance imaging (fMRI[5]) as they viewed a center of a screen where a stream of letters appeared every half second. The subjects were asked to spontaneously make the decision to press either the left or right button using their corresponding index finger (free response).

Subsequently, the volunteers were then asked to show which letter was on the screen after they pushed a button.

Analysis of the fMRI scans revealed that the brain's prefrontal and parietal cortex lit up to 10 seconds before the button was pressed, suggesting that the outcome of a decision in brain activity is encoded up to 10 seconds before it enters awareness.

In conclusion, long before you decided to push the button, your brain may have already said "click that button." **So, it may be possible that your brain "wills" an action before you are consciously aware of your will.**

Now, reflect on your habits. These are countless little actions, thoughts, and decisions you take every day that play into who you are. Yet you hardly notice them as they pass you by.

In fact, most of the time, you are unconsciously unaware of why you decide on one course of action versus another, so **it is probable that your brain may unconsciously affect your behavior much more than you probably acknowledge!**

---

[5] fMRI measures blood flow in the brain to assess brain activity.

Business Thinking

In 1926, the American writer and philosopher Will Durant, best known for his work *The Story of Civilization*,[6] would paraphrase Aristotle: "**We are what we repeatedly do… therefore excellence is not an act, but a habit.**"[7]

In this inspirational quote, the Durants set **your strategic direction for your *Warp Speed Habits* quest. You can't expect excellence on demand**. It is not something that is done infrequently or by absolute force of will. You can't just randomly improve. You don't do great work or make great decisions by accident.

This is **a journey that takes time, effort, and strategic vision**. Unfortunately, the latter happens too rarely at an individual level.

Epictetus, a Greek Stoic philosopher, had said, 1800 years earlier,

Every habit and capability is confirmed and grows in its corresponding actions, walking by walking and running by running… therefore, **if you want to do something, make a habit of it**, if you don't want to do that, don't, but make a habit of something else instead.[8]

This excerpt from an informal lecture by Epictetus sets **the tactical stage for your quest… whatever you continuously practice (good or bad) and monitor, you get better at.**

If, however, you focus only on the short term, you will squander your energy and time on in-the-moment achievements. This can lead you wide of your mark, as what will emerge from your habitual processes will differ from your intentions, as you are not guided by an explicit sense of purpose.

---

[6] Eleven volumes written over five decades in collaboration with his wife and coauthor, Ariel Durant.

[7] This quote appears in the book *The Story of Philosophy*, in which the authors narrate the work of history's greatest philosophers.

[8] From "The Discourses of Epictetus," a series of informal lectures by the Stoic philosopher Epictetus. Thought to have been written by his pupil Arrian around 108 AD.

This much-needed fusion between your strategy and your tactics is true for just about any profession or any goal for improvement that you set for yourself (see Figure I.2).

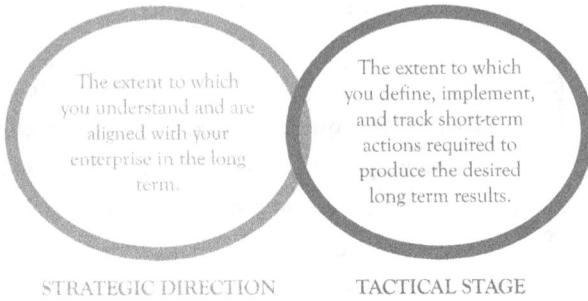

The extent to which you understand and are aligned with your enterprise in the long term.

The extent to which you define, implement, and track short-term actions required to produce the desired long term results.

STRATEGIC DIRECTION   TACTICAL STAGE

Figure I.2 Business thinking for creating habits

In your quest, from a strategic standpoint, you will understand your unique experiences and values, develop a clear vision, define strategic goals, and identify the habits you wish to build.

From a tactical perspective, you will define your objectives and tactics and implement your habits in alignment with your vision.

***

🚀 Mission 4: Reflecting Upon Strategy and Tactics

To understand the essence of strategy and tactics, take 5 to 10 minutes to reflect upon the following questions.

You may not have the replies to all of these, but do not be concerned. You will delve into these perspectives in greater detail throughout your voyages.

Strategic Perspective

- Which person do you see yourself as?
- Which person do you want to become?
- What areas do you think you excel in? Where do you need to improve?
- Will you pull out all stops, no matter what?

Tactical Perspective

- Think about your activities from the prior week, as well as those you've planned for today and the following weeks. How closely do your actions correspond to the person you'd like to be or see yourself as?
- What are you doing today that doesn't match who you are?
- Are you practicing and developing habits that will lead you toward excellence?
- Are you ready to take criticism on board and learn from others?

***

Growth Mindset for Habits

This probably is no surprise to you, but there's no such thing as an instant "Habits Growth Mindset."[9]

If you want to embrace challenges and grow in responsibilities, contribute to others, persist in the face of setbacks, commit to effort in the path to mastery, learn from criticism, and find lessons and inspiration in the success of others, you will need to build up your "Habits Growth Mindset."

Those who are the best became that way because they:

- Have a strong desire to excel.
- Believe that learning new skills is possible.
- Commit to deliberate practice and continuous learning.

How the journey of creating and changing habits begins and unfolds depends on you, but the good news is that as you start your *Warp Speed Habits* quest, you start winning, shifting away from self-doubt and procrastination and toward learning—you will be moving in the right direction!

***

---

[9] Based on Carol Dweck's Fixed and Growth Mindset model.

🚀 Mission 5: Do You Have a "Habits Growth Mindset"?

Complete the quick survey given here, selecting 1 to 4 for each statement, where 1—strongly disagree; 2—disagree; 3—agree; 4—strongly agree. The instructions in your workbook will provide a high-level assessment of the score of your survey.

1. I believe I have the potential to achieve my goals. ____
2. I enjoy taking on challenges and performing my best in every situation. ____
3. I enjoy learning new skills and believe that learning is a lifelong pursuit. ____
4. By staying focused and practicing deliberately, I can become good at a specific skill, regardless of my natural ability. ____
5. I learn from my mistakes rather than feel guilty about them. ____
6. I'm fully aware of my unique strengths and areas for improvement. ____
7. I'm not afraid to publicly admit when I've made a mistake, and work to learn from and correct it. ____

Note that the result of this assessment is for indicative purposes only.

It will help you reflect and identify areas for improvement. Always remember that anyone can develop a "habits mindset" with consistent effort and commitment.

***

Shape Your Environment

You may be unaware, but environmental context is an invisible force that helps create and maintain habits.

The immediate social, emotional, and physical environment surrounding you sets boundaries for your behaviors and can overpower your ability to act in line with your objectives, influencing the choices you make.

You've seen earlier that almost half of your daily activities are executed in the same environment. Now think about this. Are norms, information framing, loss aversion, or social pressure influencing your behaviors?

The behaviors that your environmental contexts support or discourage will probably steer the creation of your habits.

You will need to carefully design and modify your social, emotional, and physical environmental contexts where you will be creating or changing your habits.

This will allow you to leverage automatic behavioral responses based on environments that you have designed and implemented and not depend on impulsive, automatic systems.

***

🚀 Mission 6: Does Your Environment Affect Your Habits?

Take a look at the following triggers in your environment. Do they affect how you can create or change habits?

- Social triggers, for example, peer pressure?
- Emotional triggers, for example, anxiety, stress?
- Physical triggers, for example, clutter, poor organization?
- Are they helping or hurting your progress?
- Can you think of a few ways that you can change your environment to make it easier or harder to create or change habits?

***

Before completing your first voyage, let's look at the question that is probably lurking in your mind.

How Long Will I Take to Build a Habit?

I am often asked how long it takes to create a habit. Invariably, my answer is, "The average time you take to transfer habits to your subconscious mind is... well, it depends."

There are many estimates related to the time required to build habits. One of the most-cited studies presents results of 96 people choosing a daily behavior to make into a habit, for example [12]:

- Healthy eating—eating fruit with lunch.
- Drinking—drinking water with lunch.
- Exercise—running for 20 minutes before dinner.

Researchers asked participants to execute these behaviors once a day for 12 weeks in response to a trigger (an event that sets off the action).

These participants took 66 days on average to adopt new habits, but with a significant range of between 18 and 254 days for habits to become automatic.

Back to the question, "How long will I take to build a habit?"

My answer is,

Well, it depends... on the contexts of your environments, your situation, how challenging the habit is, the strength of your strategy, your level of commitment and motivation, the support you will have from other colleagues or friends, how you monitor progress, and a myriad of other factors.

And the time it takes different individuals to reach automaticity for the same habit will also be different. Various studies have shown that when in a resting state or doing various similar tasks, the brain activity patterns from one person to the next are different enough to identify individuals, much like the unique patterns of whorls and lines on their fingertips [13].

Everybody is different, with the mix of genetic and nongenetic factors influencing how your brain functions and its anatomy, resulting in distinct manners that individuals create and change habits, as well as the time required.

But is the question, "How long will I take to build a habit?" the correct question to ask? And the answer is, "No, it is not the correct question."

A (new) habit is a behavior you will want to do for years to come, not a finish line to be crossed. Achieving your strategy is a journey to the destination you choose in which you execute your tactics repeatedly until they become a constant flow of good habits. **Instead of concerning**

yourself with how long it will take to fully assimilate a habit, focus on your unique and personal quest to build your habits to achieve the change you desire.

As the novice, you have just successfully completed the first six exploratory missions in your voyage—*Brain Science, Business Thinking, Habits Mindset, and Environmental Contexts.*

During these missions, fundamental insights have come to light, and you have gained knowledge that has allowed you to understand that:

- You **are probably not effective at creating habits** consistently.
- You **need to create a dialogue between neuroscience and psychology**, as sustainable change requires a scientific understanding of the neurobiological mechanisms that are an intrinsic part of your identity.
- **Applying business thinking at a personal level is paramount** to leveraging your capability to build your habits.
- This **shift toward learning will propel you to a mindset essential for creating habits**, as you realize that the reward is not only at the destination, but also during the journey.
- You will **need to redesign your social, emotional, and physical environments** to facilitate the creation of habits.

With the brain in mind, you will be able to understand and apply the *Warp Speed Habits* strategic-tactical framework. You will build stronger habits and behaviors and grow and lead better lives, both within your organization and at a personal level.

It may not be easy, but in your *Warp Speed Habits* quest, you'll find that the knowledge you will acquire through your voyages and your missions, allied with repeated practice in using this approach, can transform your life and your brain.

There are probably few things in life as powerful as good habits. The choice is yours; this road is yours to travel, to challenge yourself to create habits and change what you repeatedly do!

As so aptly said by Santiago Ramón y Cajal, Spanish neuroscientist and Nobel Prize in physiology, **"Any man could, if he were so inclined, be the sculptor of his own brain."**

PART 2

The Scientist

A person who will gain a system of scientific knowledge covering the general laws of what makes the brain tick when building or changing habits.

Now that you have comprehended the scope of your quest and the different voyages you will need to undertake to create habits, you are ready to assume your second avatar (see Figure 2.1).

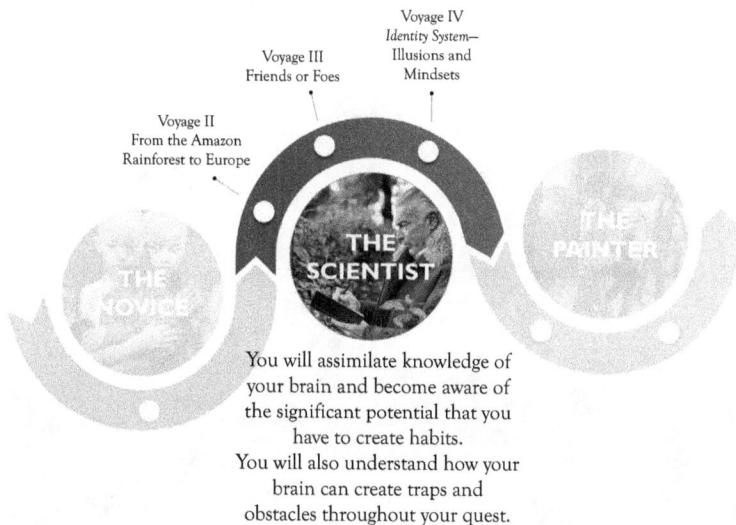

Figure 2.1 Exploring the final frontier

As the scientist, be this Albert Einstein, Marie Curie, Galileo Galilei, or any other scientist of your choice, you will go on three voyages.

During these voyages, you will execute missions that will allow you to assimilate knowledge of your brain and understand the significant potential that you have to create habits and change behaviors, to learn and grow.

You will also understand how your different brain systems affect the creation of habits, and how your *Identity System* illusion and mindset affects your work and your life.

Now that you've understood the voyages you will undertake in this part of your quest, you can assume your scientist avatar.

VOYAGE II

From the Amazon Rainforest to Europe

By constantly focusing on your thoughts, feelings, and behaviors, you can alter and improve your brain circuitry to become better suited to create habits.

As the scientist, your **objectives for this voyage** are:

⊕ **Assimilate basic knowledge of your brain,** the most complex organ in the universe.

⊕ **Become aware of the significant potential that you have** to create habits and change behaviors, to learn and grow.

⊕ Begin to **understand why your brain resists change.**

***

To achieve these objectives, you will need to execute the following four missions:

🚀 Mission 7: How Do Habits Form?
🚀 Mission 8: The Habit-Building Block
🚀 Mission 9: Flying Above the Amazon Rainforest
🚀 Mission 10: Flying Over the Mediterranean Sea by Night

***

Let's come back to the question, "What does the word 'habit' mean?"

Rarely will someone reply to this question with the following statement, "A habit is a motor or cognitive routine that is triggered by the brain in response to real or perceived triggers within specific contexts and that, once triggered, is completed with unconscious competence."

From the aforementioned phrase, what stands out are the words "unconscious competence," but what do these words mean in relation to habit formation?

You will now move on to your **first preparatory mission for this voyage, to understand how habits form from a brain-based perspective**.

Habits Formation Matrix: An Overview

Habits form over an identifiable series of four stages along the **Habits Formation Matrix**[1] (see Figure II.1), which compares the levels of competence achieved in executing a habit with the levels of consciousness required to execute the said habit.

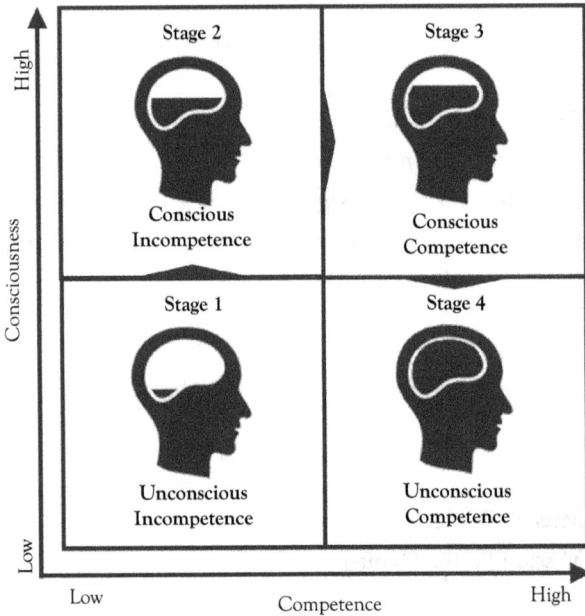

Figure II.1 Habits Formation Matrix

The horizontal axis represents the level of competence (from low to high), while the vertical axis represents the level of consciousness (also from low to high).

---

[1] Adapted from the Conscious Competence Ladder and Matrix developed in the 1970s by Noel Burch of Gordon Training International, to include a brain-based perspective in the habit creation process.

As you begin to create habits, you will start at the stage of Unconscious Incompetence and move through the intermediate stages before reaching the stage of Unconscious Competence, where you execute the habit automatically.

Before reviewing the Habits Formation Matrix in more detail, take five minutes to complete the following mission.

***

🚀 Mission 7: How Do Habits Form?

Match the corresponding descriptions (A to D) shown in Table II.1 to each of the four stages shown in Figure II.1. The answers are provided in your workbook.

Table II.1 Habits matrix stages description

Descriptions	Stages (1 to 4)
A • Medium computational cost • Reflective • Partially active deliberation	
B • High computational cost • Reflective • Active deliberation • Adaptive flexibility	
C • High computational efficiency • Reflexive • High level of automaticity • Inflexible	
D • Nonexistent computational cost	

***

To better understand the Habits Formation Matrix, imagine that you've just successfully learned a process that required the use of new application software.

You started at **stage 1: Unconscious Incompetence,** the stage of unawareness, where you did not have knowledge of the process or the application and it didn't matter to you, or you may have thought that the skill looked easy enough to master.

At this stage, your cognitive computational cost (use of mental energy) was low, as you toyed with the advantages of implementing the process and application.

In **stage 2: Conscious Incompetence,** you defined the specific goal of implementing the new process and associated application within your work routines.

You reflected on what you did not know, and as you tried to make sense of the procedures and functions of the menus, you felt awkwardness and uncertainty.

In this stage, your cognitive computational cost was increasing.

In **stage 3: Conscious Competence,** you became competent and excited, as you performed several functions of the process and navigated the application.

You were still fully aware of what you were doing, with flexibility in the manner that you learned and executed the activities, but a significant amount of mental energy was still being consumed as you paid careful attention to executing the process and each minor accomplishment achieved.

From a brain perspective, this means that repeated behavior was being incrementally absorbed by the cognitive processing units of your procedural memory [3].[2]

In **stage 4: Unconscious Competence,** the habit became a part of you, as you used the application to perform the new process without thinking twice, no longer spending conscious resources on this activity.

Repeated behavior led to full absorption of the habit, as all relevant neural systems worked together to execute the habit automatically. The habit became embedded in your brain's neural networks.

---

[2] Procedural memory is a subset of implicit memory. It enables you to perform everyday physical activities, such as walking and riding a bike, without having to give it much thought.

With this level of behavior automaticity, you will perform specific types of tasks without conscious awareness of prior experiences or without occupying the mind with the low-level details needed.

From the matrix presented, you can see that as you move from stage 1 to stage 4, by repeating a behavior, you are moving from intentional action to behavior automaticity.

The knowledge that you've acquired from **the Habits Formation Matrix has allowed you to recognize your cognitive computational costs, emotions, and (in)flexibility as you go through building or changing habits**. This will help reduce the strain and challenges inherent in creating habits.

In the **following exploratory mission, you will understand neurons**—one of the key building blocks of your nervous system that runs throughout your body—and their fundamental contribution to habit formation.

The Basic Building Block of Habits

Imagine that, after long, hard days at the office, you've gotten into the habit of running or walking before dinner.

Your ability to process this routine, from putting on your running shoes to running or walking on the track, and so much more, all begins with the fundamental units of the brain, the nerve cell, or neuron, and the glial cell, or glia [14]. Together, they form ensembles called neural circuits that interconnect to one another to form large-scale brain networks.

As you start running or walking, your neural circuits perform various functions:

- Your sensory systems, such as your visual system, reports information about the state of the environment, for example, what you see on and around the track in front of you.
- Your motor system organizes and generates actions, such as controlling muscles throughout your body, including your legs and arms.
- Associational systems allow you to think about what you are doing and remember what has happened through brain

functions such as perception, attention, memory, emotions, language, and thinking.

• Your nervous system also controls fundamental functions, like breathing and regulating your body temperature.

In short, your nervous system detects what is going on around and inside you, decides how you should act, adjusts the state of your internal organs, and provides "higher-order" brain functions.

But how do these circuits communicate and interact?

Although neurons and the communication networks they form are complex, their basic structure is quite simple. Using the analogy of a tree, given the almost **tree-like structure of a neuron** (see Figure II.2), you can think of a neuron as forming four basic parts:

1. A *cell body*, which can be compared to the base of the tree, contains the nucleus.
2. Long *dendrites*, which can be compared to the roots of the tree, extend from the cell body. It is these dendrites that receive the signals from other neurons.
3. An *axon*, which can be compared to the trunk of the tree, is a long, thin structure that extends from the cell body.

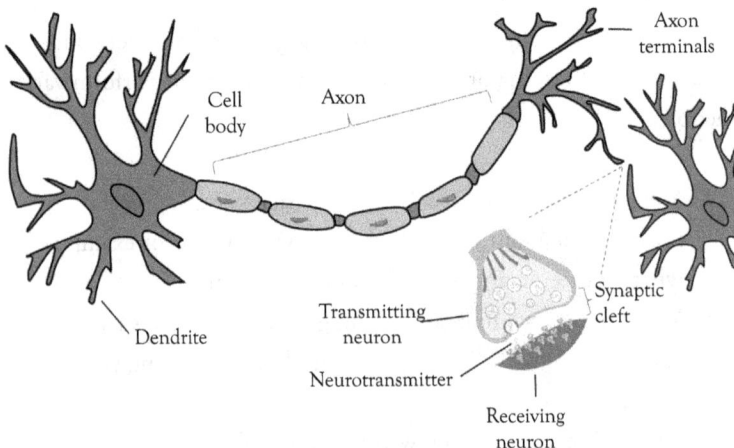

Figure II.2 Neuron—the habit-building block

4. Near the end, the axon branches off and forms *axon terminals*, which can be compared to the branches of the tree. The axon conducts or passes on signals to its terminals, and chemicals are transported to other neurons through these terminals.

You can think of the information flowing through your nervous system in the following manner [15]:

- An electrical discharge runs from the base (cell body) of the tree (neuron) along the length of its trunk (axon) and through to the tips of widespread branches (axon terminals).
- The impulse activates electrically charged neurotransmitters. These are chemicals produced in the cell body of the neuron, transported, and stored in the axon terminal.[3]
- These neurotransmitters are released by the tips of the widespread branches (axon terminals) and cross a juncture, or synaptic cleft, between neurons (see Figure II.2).
- These messengers attach themselves to the binding receptors of an extensive system of roots (thin filaments called dendrites) of the second tree (neuron).[4]
- Upon docking, the neurotransmitter alters the electrical charge at the edge of the neuron and sparks a new electrical impulse.
- If enough neurotransmitters have bound to the receptor, generating enough electrical potential, a signal is conducted through the second neuron (tree) until it reaches the axon terminal (branches), with the same process being repeated.[5]

---

[3] Neurotransmitters are important to boost and balance signals in the brain and to keep the brain and body functioning. For example, dopamine and oxytocin are two of over 100 neurotransmitters discovered by scientists [14]; the former plays a role in pleasure, motivation, and learning, and the latter in bonding and trust.
[4] Note that specific neurons can only dock at specifically shaped docking sites.
[5] For neurons to function well, the glial cells play a fundamental role in regulating metabolic equilibrium. There are five types of glial cells, each with a specific function, but you can think of the glia as caretakers of the trees, protecting and supporting neurons by supplying them with nutrients and oxygen, insulating them from one another, destroying pathogens, and cleaning up dead neurons.

How do these "tree messengers" communicate when executing or creating a habit?

As impulses pass among these complex chains in your central nervous system, they form networks that specialize in performing a myriad of specific tasks.

When triggered by an external or internal cue, such as events (you've seen your running shoes and have decided to go for a run), emotions, or thoughts, a neuron will transmit signals to a target cell, which can be a different neuron, muscle cell, or gland cell.

Through this continuous process, the message from the brain travels down the nerves to the muscles in the hand and tells the muscle what to do—pick up the running shoe, slip in your foot, tie the shoelace, and so on.

Neurons not only help manage automatic responses such as breathing and heart rate, but also have **psychological functions such as learning, remembering experiences, managing mood**, fear, pleasure, and happiness, and **play a fundamental role in building and changing habits.**

***

🚀 Mission 8: The Habit-Building Block

A quick check on how well you've grasped this information.

Complete the phrase given next with the following options (see workbook for answers):

(synaptic clefts/electricity/habits/chemical/networks]

In short, all **information processed by the brain is nothing more than** [a] _____ **passing through neurons** and chains of neurons, pausing only to be **converted into** [b] _____ **messengers** and **leaping across** [c] _____.

Together, **neurons and glia form** [d] _____ that specialize in performing specific functions and playing a fundamental role in building and changing [e] _____.

Now imagine this continuous process across billions of cells, these tree-like structures connecting and "talking" to other tree-like structures, within a "brain jungle."

***

The Amazon Rainforest

The adult brain weighs in at roughly 3.1 pounds and has between 85 million and 90 billion neurons and more or less the same number of nonneuronal cells, including glia [16].[6]

That's approximately 180 billion cells... wow, a number difficult to imagine! We humans are smart, but when it comes to understanding and handling excessively large numbers, we have an overly positive assessment of our capabilities.

To understand the sheer complexity of what you will see and experience as you travel within the *Final Frontier*, we will once again use the analogy of the tree, so 180 billion cells equates to 180 billion trees.

It is time for another mission, where in your scientist avatar, you will captain the vessel *Brainship Enterprise I*. One small point, to execute these missions, you and your vessel will be shrunk to microscopic size, but only for one hour.[7] Use this time wisely as you execute the following three missions as the scientist!

***

🚀 Mission 9: Flying Above the Amazon Rainforest

You receive instructions on how to pilot *Brainship Enterprise I* and are set to go. On board, you are miniaturized to about the size of a microbe and injected into a brain. Suited up, you are beamed out of the vessel and find yourself next to a Wimba tree[8] (aka neuron in this voyage). Think of the Wimba tree as a type of neuron—this is easier than trying to imagine a neuron.

Now, imagine someone else peering through a high-resolution microscope—the neurons and glial cells are microscopically small[9]—at

---

[6] To date, the glia to neuron ratio is still under debate, with the most compelling evidence for a 1:1 ratio mentioned in the study cited [16] used as a reference point.

[7] Loosely based on the 1966 American science fiction story *Fantastic Voyage*, by O. Klement and J. Bixby.

[8] These trees are among the tallest in this rainforest, growing up to 55 meters in height.

[9] Neurons vary from 5 to 150 micrometers or micron, while astrocytes, the largest of glial cells, have an average diameter of 40 to 50 micrometers.

the small part of this "brain-jungle" where you've just landed. They adjust
the microscope to magnify this part of the "brain-jungle," bring it into
focus, peek in between the leaves of the trees, and there you are, standing
next to a Wimba tree in the middle of the Amazon rainforest.

Remember, the roots of the tree are the dendrites of the neuron, the
trunk of the tree is the axon, the tree branches are the axon terminals, and
the glia protects the tree.

You can touch the Wimba "neuron tree" and feel the pulsating energy
as it communicates with other trees.

Look up. You will see the canopy of the rainforest composed of the
tallest trees, ranging from 20 to over 80 meters in height [17].

You beam yourself back on board *Brainship Enterprise I*, and back at the
commands, you rise above the trees. The jungle-like richness and density of
this upper region of trees make it almost impossible to see the sky, but you
push through and suddenly, you see the trees extending through to the hori-
zon. It seems endless, the Amazon rainforest, a vast, complex ocean of trees.

You push higher and higher above Brazil until you see the basin
encompassing the 2.12 million square miles covered by the Amazon
rainforest, spread across nine countries (see Figure II.3).[10]

The Amazon rainforest in Brazil alone has approximately 250 billion
trees.[11]

Now imagine with the technology you have aboard your vessel that
you can scan and unfold the 3.1-pound brain, the way you unfold a map,
and place this scanned version of your brain over a map of the Amazon
rainforest (remember, one tree equates to one neuron).

The scanned version of your brain map will fall just within the borders
of the Brazilian Amazon rainforest. This comparison begins to give you
an inkling of the dimension of 180 billion neurons and glial cells and the
sheer complexity of your brain!

***

---

[10] Brazil, Ecuador, Venezuela, Suriname, Peru, Colombia, Bolivia, Guyana, and
French Guiana.
[11] Based on an estimate by the author, considering that the Amazon rainforest has 390 billion trees, and that Brazil covers 64 percent of the Amazon
rainforest [18].

Figure II.3 The Amazon rainforest

Flying to Southern Europe

It is, however, not the number of neurons that matters as much as the number and frequency of synaptic connections between them that make the brain amazing.

This "pulsing activity" of approximately 90 billion neurons, firing electrical impulses and discharging chemical messages across synapses, forges trillions of connections in this complex network.

These 90 billion neurons, finding, coupling, and disengaging from one another, are what allows your brain to hold representations of anything from as simple as an orange; your memories; thoughts as uneventful as "I need a cup of coffee"; to the most complex of thoughts such as "I feel, therefore I am"[12]; and ultimately, your consciousness.

To understand the dynamics of this "communication network," you are going to continue your mission of imagination, captaining the turbine-engine vessel *Brainship Enterprise I.*

---

[12] Neuroscientist António Damásio on consciousness and how the feeling-tone of the body underscores the symphony of the mind.

***

🚀 Mission 10: Flying Over the Mediterranean Sea by Night

The night sky is setting, and you decide that you want to explore another part of your brain. You travel at warp speed across to the Mediterranean Sea, just off the coast of Spain.

It is now evening in Europe. You look down and see billions of neurons pulsing, as they communicate with each other.

Visualizing the neurons communicating below, imagine the different frequencies and intensities of this network represented by the lights of villages, towns, and cities.

You make out the glow of the city nightlights inland and along the coasts of Italy, France, Spain, and Portugal.

There are places where neurons are starting to exchange information. Villages and towns are coming alive.

There are major and minor clusters of neurons, cities with small clusters, and capitals with major clusters of communication.

You will notice solid lines crossing the countries, with clusters of neurons connected to other clusters, and major cities connected by networks of highways.

The sparsely lit interiors of these countries where communication is minimal and areas that are largely void of illumination will begin to catch your eye.

You can compare these networks to the tangled network formed between your brain cells, with neurons wired to tens of thousands of other neurons.

Look at your virtual brain map. You can see this action in real time. Every time you move, think, feel, act, or remember, you will access or create neural pathways of connections involving a multitude of neurons, just as you have seen the villages, towns, and cities of all sizes lighting up.

***

Creating Cities and Superhighways

What research has shown is that **creating and changing habits, leading to adjustments in the brain's structure and to the shape of neurons and dendrites, depend on this constant communication activity at synapses.**

This is described by the Hebbian theory or Hebb's law, "cells that fire together, wire together." This theory aims to explain how repeated experience leads to neural pathways developing, that is, as communication between neurons becomes frequent, the connection becomes stronger and faster.

This law is best evoked by the passage in Donald Hebb's book, *The Organization of Behavior: A Neuropsychological Theory*, which states that:

> When an axon of cell A is near enough to excite cell B and repeatedly or persistently takes part in firing it, some growth process or metabolic change takes place in one or both cells, such that A's efficiency, as one of the cells firing B, is increased.

The likelihood of an action-response[13] becoming a habit will depend on the efficiency and effectiveness of neuron A in firing and exciting neuron B. If neuron A is successful, the two neurons lock together, leading to a metabolic change in one or both neurons.

Practicing a new behavior under the right conditions, as referred to by Michael Merzenich, the father of plasticity, **can change hundreds of millions and possibly billions of the connections** between the nerve cells in our neural pathways.

By mobilizing your thoughts and practicing new ways of thinking, you can reshape the communication between your neurons, alter connections in your networks, and change the structure of your brain and even the way your brain works.

Brain circuits will become strengthened, habits created and more ingrained in response to recurring and similar situations, events, thoughts, or emotions. A faint trail will become a well-traveled hiking path, the hiking path will become a well-worn pathway with high foot traffic, villages will become towns, towns will become cities, and cities will grow with interconnecting highways to other cities.

This amazing quality of the brain, known as neuroplasticity [19], is the innate ability of your brain to learn and adapt to your environment

---

[13] Recall that the action-response is one of the four components of habits.

and change the strength of specific connections, making them either stronger or weaker with each repeated activity it performs.[14]

By constantly focusing on your thoughts, feelings, and behaviors, you can alter and improve your brain circuitry to become better suited to create habits.

Many studies in neuropsychology have shown that experts who started learning their profession in childhood or who have had intensive training and practice present structural differences in their brains as compared to nonexperts. Neuronal activity differs depending on the functions executed and the respective ability of the individual.

For example:

- London cab drivers have larger hippocampi (part of the brain involved in spatial navigation) than their peers who don't engage in these complex travel tasks. A longer duration in this profession is also associated with increasing hippocampal size [20].
- Musicians' neuronal activity is different depending on the instrument being played and on the related expertise [21].
- Yoga practitioners, when compared to control subjects, exhibit greater gray matter volume differences observed in the left hippocampus, suggesting an association between regular long-term yoga practice and differences in structure and function of specific brain regions involved in executive function, specifically working memory [22].

You have just successfully completed your first voyage as the scientist. During your missions, you have understood that:

- **With 90 billion neurons, supported by 90 billion glia, firing trillions of constant connections, the options you have to learn, experience events, and encode and process information in your brain are limitless!**

---

[14] First described by Polish neuroscientist Jerzy Konorski in 1948, the word neuroplasticity is derived from "neuro," as pertaining to a nerve or nerves or the nervous system, from Greek neura; and "plasticity," as pertaining to the characteristic of plastic quality, from Greek plastikos, meaning "formed" or "molded."

- It is through your **mental activity that you can become the sculptor of your brain**, as opposed to your mental activity only being a product of your brain.
- This is precisely **one of the reasons why resistance to create or change habits is higher.** Your current habits have carved deep pathways in your brain, and if your brain doesn't get the correct, focused, and constant input, the corresponding conversations between neurons across the network will be insufficient, your current habits will dominate, and your new habits infrastructure won't develop properly.

The good news is that **with *Warp Speed Habits*, you will master the process of habit formation, and the sparsely lit walking trails you choose to develop will become major cities and superhighways with intense traffic**, as you leave no road unfinished.

VOYAGE III

Friends or Foes

Habit is either the best of servants or the worst of masters.
—Nathaniel Emmons

In your second voyage as the scientist, **your objectives** are:

⊕ **Understand the different intricacies of your brain systems** and how these operate in creating habits.
⊕ Comprehend **how these systems are interlinked and how they affect the creation of habits**.

***

To achieve these objectives, you will need to execute one mission:

🚀 Mission 11: A Balancing Act

***

You have an enormous transformative potential to learn, adapt, improve, and grow. Why, then, is it extremely challenging to build or change habits?

Why are you sometimes able to create superhighways, and in other cases, all your efforts to build new brain infrastructure fail miserably?

How and why do your current habits exert such a tremendous pull over you, positively and negatively? Why do your old habits fall so easily back into place?

To understand this phenomenon, you will explore some of the brain systems[1] where it is likely that habits originate.

---

[1] Systems that describe the generic functioning of the brain in relation to the creation of habits.

Note that it is less important that you know the names of where habits emanate from and more important to realize how the brain systems work together in building habits.

With this basic understanding of the inner workings of the brain involved in creating habits, you will understand why you feel the way you do as habits form and why your current habits exert such an intense pull over you.

This knowledge will help you mitigate the risks of being seriously sabotaged and compromised as you create habits.

Exploring the Final Frontier Systems

On board *Brainship Enterprise I*, you will travel to different brain systems to understand how they contribute and impact the creation of habits.

The knowledge you acquire will help you understand and evaluate these systems. Are they friends or foes? Or, after your mission, will you have a different perspective of how these systems can support you in creating and changing habits?

The systems you will travel to include the executive, habits, risk analysis, learning, and reward systems (see Figure III.1).

The Executive System

You've just reached the executive system[2] or prefrontal cortex (PFC), located behind the forehead.

Scientists derived the term executive system from the higher-order functions of this part of the brain. This system houses abilities including:

- Strategy definition and being goal oriented
- Planning, short-term thinking, and being organized and productive
- Providing impulse control and regulating complex emotions
- Communicating with others, being socially responsible, and other more sophisticated social interactions

---

[2] Also known as the executive center.

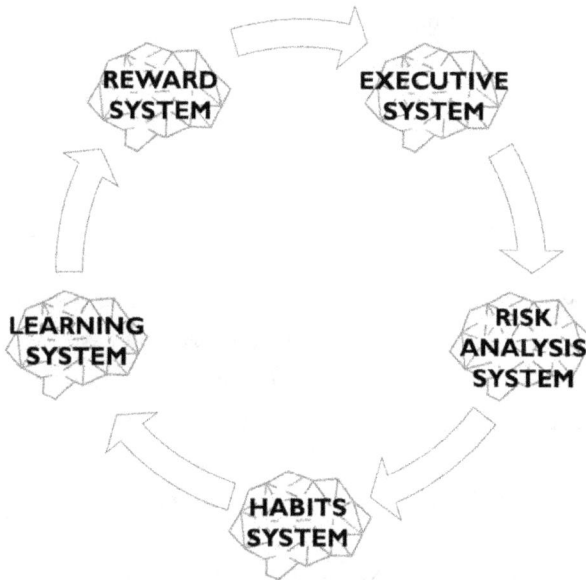

Figure III.1 The final frontier systems

Clocking in at an age of approximately 200,000 years [23], compared to the first brain structure that appeared over 500 million years ago [24], the executive system was the last major brain region to develop during human evolutionary history.[3]

Making up over 10 percent of the volume in the brain [25], this system is the "baby" of the brain and has some surprising limitations, which may result in fewer resources for the higher-order functions.

- It is energy intensive, using up a significant part of the brain's glucose and oxygen resources when active [26].
- It can only hold about four pieces of information at any one time [27].
- While it can help you hold diverse blocks of information in your mind, it can only process information serially. Your brain does not let you perform more than one conscious process without your performance being affected [28].

---

[3] The dominant view on the origin of human culture is that modern humans originated about 200,000 years ago.

- Constantly bombarded with internal and external distractions, it is easily stimulated. To manage these distractions, a higher energy consumption of oxygenated glucose is used [28].
- If you are tired, hungry, angry, lonely, or stressed out, the probability of your executive system going "offline" is highly likely [29].

Your **executive system packs a powerful punch** and plays a fundamental role in creating and changing habits. As you have seen, though, **it is extremely fragile** and depends on the correct functioning of its neural network connections, which are highly sensitive to its neurochemical environment.

To onboard habits, you will need to maintain a healthy executive system.

With this high-level summary of the executive system in mind, it is now time to travel to the risk analysis system.

The Risk Analysis System

Your brain is much more than a thought-processing communication network. Your risk analysis system or warning center's governing foundation is to keep you alive [30], by scanning your environment every fifth of a second, below your conscious awareness.

"Wired" to avoid threats and seek rewards, it processes the former far faster and in a more intense manner than the latter. These threat avoidance and reward seeking lead to habits being created.

Constantly avoiding a person who evokes conflict and competition, a looming crisis, a tight deadline that provokes anxiety, or building a habit that disrupts the status quo may make you feel uncomfortable.

If you perceive these situations as stressful or even mildly stressful, your brain jumps into action and will attempt to avoid this threat by triggering the neurotransmitter norepinephrine[4].

---

[4] Norepinephrine is the term usually preferred in the United States, whereas noradrenaline is more commonly used in the United Kingdom.

This switch opens the floodgate of adrenaline, floods your blood-stream, and readies you for action, at the same time disengaging flow of energy to your executive system.

If uncomfortable situations like these are not managed correctly, psychological and social survival will dominate your thoughts and negatively affect your executive system. Intense situations may even increase the likelihood of your risk analysis system becoming oversensitive.

The result is neural connections becoming dysfunctional, and you get a powerful impression that something is wrong (see Figure III.2).

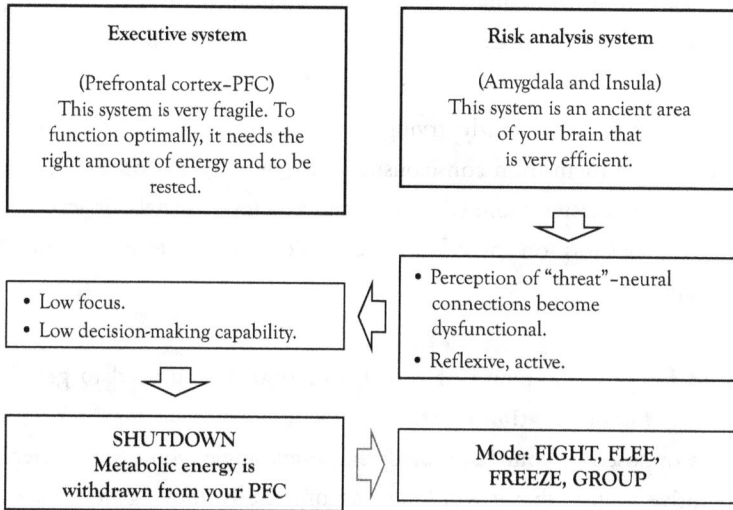

Figure III.2 The sensitive risk analysis system in action

Faced with **building a habit, you will push your brain beyond the boundaries of your comfort zone, moving into unexplored neural areas as you try to create new pathways.** In these perceived threat situations, your brain may "push" you back into consolidated neural pathways.

To create or change habits, you will need to make the process feel comfortable, so that your brain recognizes the reward-seeking patterns that will facilitate creating habits.

Now that you've grasped how your risk analysis system functions, it is time to beam back on board and set a course for the habits system.

The Habits System

You review your research notes and see that this system is comprised by the basal ganglia, a region at the base of the brain.

Responsible for automatic thoughts and movements, the habits system works wonders.

It is an efficient pattern-repeater that processes thoughts, feelings, and behavioral responses spontaneously and effortlessly. This system allows you to allocate your attention to other tasks, by **reducing cognitive load and freeing up mental capacity to save time and energy** [30].

Gerard Roth, a German biologist and brain researcher, sums this up [31] when he tells us that:

> The brain is constantly trying to automate processes, thereby dispelling them from consciousness; in this way, its work will be completed faster, more effectively, and at a lower metabolic level. Consciousness, on the other hand, is slow, subject to error, and "expensive."

To fully use the power of your habits system, you need to **get the process of habit creation right.**

As opposed to your brain analyzing every angle, you need to create "cognitive scripts" that it will follow automatically, moving from *unconscious incompetence* to *unconscious competence* rapidly, skipping the process of trial and error!

How can you do this, you wonder?

While some experiences are short-lived, your habits need to be transformed into lasting memories and behaviors. To do this, you will need to get your memory, and the cognitive, motor, and affective components of learning, to work together, transforming your learning into sustainable habits.

Eric R. Kandel, Nobel Prize winner for research on molecular foundations of memory, segregates these two dimensions in the following manner: **"Learning is how you acquire new information about the world, and memory is how you store that information over time."**

How you hardwire your actions and thoughts is fundamental to create habits.

It is now time to travel to the learning system.

The Learning System

Instinctively, you know you need to have self-control and be focused as you learn to create or change habits. As Amy Arnsten, American neuro-scientist, points out,

> The loss of prefrontal function only occurs when we feel out of control. It is the prefrontal cortex itself that is determining if we are in control or not. Even if we have the illusion that we are in control, our cognitive functions are preserved.

But how can you ensure that you are in control when you are learning to create habits?

Amy Arnsten answers this question through the inverted-U model of arousal[5] [29] (see Figure III.3).

This model describes what you will have experienced before:

- With a **low level of alertness** (on the left side of the inverted-U), you will not be "stretched." You will **easily become bored, distracted, tired, and inactive.**

  Norepinephrine and dopamine[6] will not be triggered, leading to **weak prefrontal connections** and impaired cognitive abilities.

---

[5] Based on the Yerkes–Dodson law, the inverted U-model shows the relationship between stress and task performance.

[6] Norepinephrine (or noradrenaline) acts as a stress hormone and neurotransmitter—you need just the right amount to "energize" yourself in moments of stressful situations. Dopamine, on the other hand, is a neurotransmitter that motivates or propels an individual's behavior toward or away from a specific action.

This will result in **poor performance and behavior that is reflexive**, disorganized, and forgetful. In this state, you will demonstrate a lack of inhibition and empathy.

- With just the **right level of alertness** at the top of the curve, the **cognitive performance of your executive system will be at its peak**. In this state, you will feel safe, in control, and alert, and you will achieve optimal arousal and performance.

  In this focused and almost effortless "toward state," you will be more thoughtful and reflective. You will have a better working memory, be more attentive, organized, empathetic, and control your impulses.

  This will persist as long as small, constant bursts of norepinephrine and dopamine are in balance, strengthening prefrontal connections and improving prefrontal network triggering.

- From this tipping point, with **too much stretch**, the two neurotransmitters become unbalanced, and your executive system finds it "hard to think." Your **performance becomes impaired**, leading to uncontrollable stress, anxiety, poor impulse control, lack of empathy, poor decision making, and poor memory.

To operate efficiently and effectively, the learning system needs just the right balance of the neurotransmitters dopamine and norepinephrine.

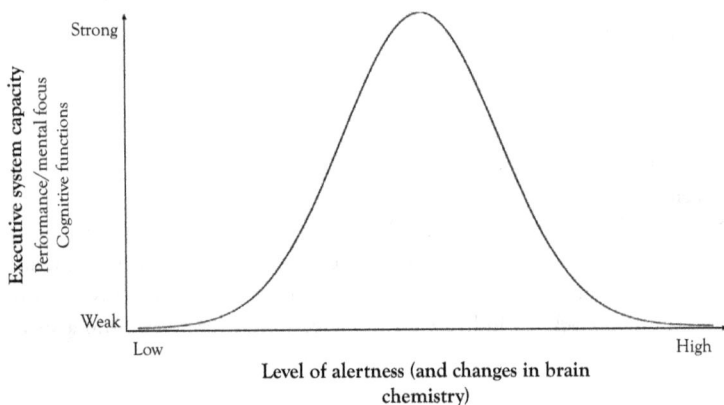

Figure III.3 Inverted-U model of arousal

Norepinephrine will strengthen the relevant executive system network connectivity, while dopamine will help maintain focus and block distraction in relation to your goals [32].

Balanced, the neurotransmitters will increase the undivided attention of your habits system, ensuring consolidation of information from short-term to long-term memory; too intense, and your system becomes stressed and out of control; too little leads to boredom and fatigue [32, 33].

The art involved is for you to understand how to achieve your optimal stretch zone.

The Reward System

You have now reached your reward system. Note you have little time left before reverting to normal size. At this stage, you will only be able to grasp essential information in relation to this system. In your maestro avatar, you will review this subject when you explore the reward and craving components of the *Habits Quartet*.

What you need to understand is that **this region of the brain is focused on self-preservation and instant gratification**. It is activated by experiences that are rewarding.

As you saw in your maiden voyage, you are swayed by the inputs you receive from your environment. Your rewards and cravings may be influenced by the related momentary and fluctuating signals generated by your brain in response to these inputs.

This system is intimately connected to your habit system, to encourage a repetition of rewarding behaviors—what is pleasurable is remembered by this system [30].

This is useful to remember as you create or change habits.

***

🚀 Mission 11: A Balancing Act

In your travels to the Amazon rainforest and southern Europe, you realized the phenomenal potential you have to learn, adapt, build habits, and grow.

In your third voyage, you discovered how your different brain systems operate and interact and that the challenges of creating or changing habits from a brain perspective are significant.

Knowing these systems and the neuroscience of habit formation is fundamental for those wanting to build habits.

In the following mission, you will recap on your understanding. You should complete the spaces in the paragraphs below with the names of the different systems—the executive, risk analysis, habits, and learning systems. Answers are provided in your workbook.

You've understood that although your (a) _____ has powerful functions, it also has surprising limitations in certain types of mental tasks. This system tires easily and consumes high levels of metabolic energy.

When not constantly oxygenated and rested, this system may become the bottleneck of the brain.

You've seen that your executive and (b) _____ interact when you are overwhelmed. This happens when you lack self-confidence, are affected by the opinions of other people, experience uncomfortable feelings, or as you try to create habits.

In these situations, your sensitive (c) _____ works in close unison with the (d) _____ to ensure your momentary survival. Together, these systems give you a sense of safety, comfort, or relief, no matter the potential future costs.

The former captures stimuli and processes information from the environment, including images, verbal interactions, emotional reactions, and body sensations. The latter follows the existing consolidated pathways of current habits.

When your (e) _____ or (f) _____ are not engaged to make choices, learn, or overcome distractions when creating or changing habits, your sensitive (g) _____ will take over. This will result in habitual behavior that lives within the (h) _____.

The latter two systems are highly efficient. Their routines have become wired into your brain without you realizing it, and this can lead to devastating consequences.

When faced with these threats, your (i) _____ is activated, sliding you back into the thicker and stronger neural pathways of your current habits. The incipient pathways you are attempting to create will simply be overridden.

Though you might think that the habits system will take away your freedom to choose, the fact is that you cannot function without it.

As your habits system is stable, it "motivates" you to act when you are low on willpower, stressed, or not able to deliberate on responses. This system will protect you from impulses or random events, providing you with predetermined action-responses or mental solutions to recurring complex problems [6].

When in command, your "educated" (j) _____ and (k) _____ can perform actions and take decisions with "conscious awareness," driving the creation of productive habits.

In these situations, the potential choices and decisions you make are based on the information you are receiving from your brain.

This is where your consciousness, your mind, comes into play. This is where you act reflectively, consider different options, weigh the short-term rewards versus the long-term benefits, and take a more strategic and tactical approach to creating habits.

***

You have just successfully completed your second voyage as the scientist. You now understand that:

- It is not about playing the systems against each other; it is not about "friends or foes"; it is **about ensuring an optimum level of equilibrium**, a balancing act you will need to maintain **between the different systems**.
  - The quick, necessary, and energy-efficient actions originate in the **risk analysis, habits, and reward systems**, which ensure transitory survival and instant gratification. It is these **automatic responses that may not help you grow and impede your progress toward achieving your goals**.
  - The longer-term decisions and learning within the **executive and learning systems** you need to get right, by **understanding the limitations and needs of these systems**, and your brain needs to conserve energy by "pushing" your mental maps and habits into your habits system.

VOYAGE IV

Identity System—Illusions and Mindsets

Becoming is better than being.

—Carol Dweck

As the scientist, your **objectives for this voyage**, complemented with the information collated from the prior two voyages, are:

- ⊕ Reflect on the **inner workings of your brain systems and their connection to your *Identity System*.**
- ⊕ Understand **how your *Identity System* illusion and mindset affect the creation of habits.**

***

To achieve these objectives, you will execute two missions:

- 🚀 Mission 12: *Identity System* Illusion
- 🚀 Mission 13: Are You Growth or Fixed Mindset?

***

Back at the office, sitting in your chair (you've reverted to your normal size), you reflect upon your recent voyages and missions.

The Inner Workings—A Reflection

You have understood how biology and the environment have interacted over millions of years in complex ways to shape and sculpt your interconnected brain systems.

Your brain functions and processes have been molded through evolutive, selective, and adaptive threat–reward, energy-efficient, and predictive, if somewhat flawed, mechanisms.

These same brain systems, hidden from your awareness, instinctively and constantly circumvent threats and defend deep-rooted habits. They define your perspectives of good and bad or right and wrong, and create social and emotional comfort zones and seemingly rational defensive borders around these.

Shaped by experiences and events, your comfort zones have developed along the path of your childhood and adulthood. These zones ultimately mold your habits, patterns of thoughts and perceptions, feelings and behaviors, core values, beliefs, mindsets, and preferences, defining who you are, your *Identity System*.

With this reflection in mind, you are now ready for two further missions, *Identity System Illusion*, and *Identity System Mindset*, which together with *The Inner Workings* of your brain, further impact and mold your *Identity System*.

Identity System Illusion

Your habits have shaped your *Identity System* to where it has become tightly fused.

As you attempt to create habits, your **risk analysis and habits systems will confound you by seeking to confirm and validate your *Identity System* with your everyday experiences**.

When asked about it at any point in our lives, we believe we have changed significantly up to the present moment but will not substantially change in the years ahead [34].

Researchers have not studied the reason for this psychological illusion in depth, but when we attempt to create habits, our brain may look inwardly at the beliefs of our *Identity System*, to make sense of who we are.

***

🚀 Mission 12: Identity System Illusion

To understand this illusion, you will carry out a mission of reflection. Take 10 minutes and respond to the following two questions in your workbook.

- What changes in your *Identity System* have you felt in yourself in the last 10 years?
- In terms of your *Identity System*, what are the changes you foresee in yourself in the next 10 years?

***

While it was probably easy to answer the first question, you may have felt difficulty in answering the second question.

You answered your first question through a reconstructive process. You noted down changes based on interpretations of your experiences and autobiographical memories [34], validated over time through similar situations.

This invariably produces flawed results, as we are not accurate observers of our memories, and we may skew what we document, influenced in part by the need to feel socially desirable, and by regarding our beliefs as truths or facts.

This misplaced ease with which you view your *Identity System* in retrospection may lead you to stay within your comfort zones. Your beliefs have become clear and vivid, but potentially inaccurate images of your memories and history. These are thoughts you have thought, and emotions you have felt, but right or wrong, they are strong convictions at best.

If your view of your past may be biased, then your view of the future is even more fraught with danger.

When you answered the second question, you probably had difficulty in attempting to view the person you want to become and the habits you wish to create. As physicist Niels Bohr (a contemporary and collaborator of Einstein) said, "Prediction is difficult, especially about the future."

You were probably only able to sketch hazy images of your future. This difficulty may arise because you are satisfied with your current state of being and are unconsciously incompetent as to your potential opportunities. Or you may have difficulty in predicting how you will change, given that your neural pathways for conducting this type of exercise are nonexistent or faint at best.

This flawed ease with which you portray your current *Identity System* and the difficulty in imagining a new one may confuse you to think that creating habits is improbable (see Figure IV.1).

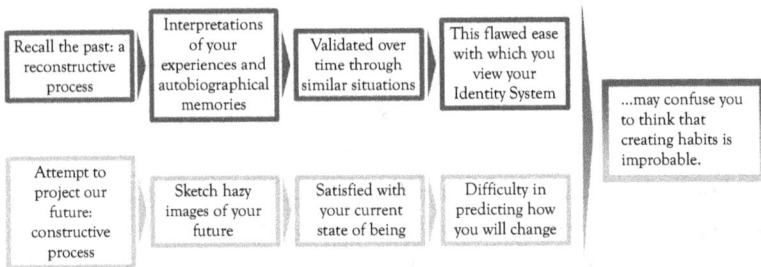

Figure IV.1 A psychological illusion

As you continue your quest, you need to bear in mind that you may unconsciously be opting to protect your *Identity System* and are invariably creating a psychological illusion.

Identity System Mindset

The hand you've been dealt till now has stacked the chips against you. The hand you deal yourself next may increase or reduce these odds.

In your first voyage, you briefly covered Carol Dweck's research that shows how most people's brains can be described as having a fixed or a growth mindset [2].

A growth mindset embodies the concept that, with enough time, focused effort, and discipline, most competencies and endeavors are learnable and achievable. A fixed mindset characterizes people as being set in their ways, with a less positive perspective about effort (see Figure IV.2).

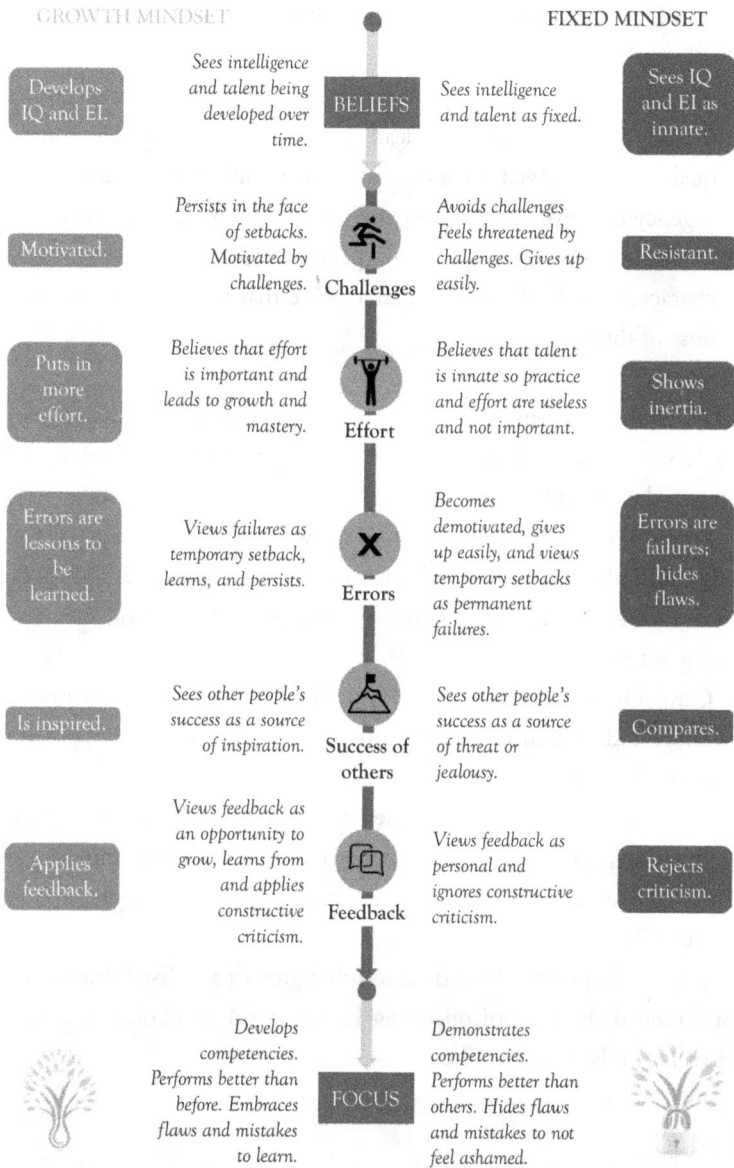

GROWTH MINDSET		FIXED MINDSET

GROWTH MINDSET   **FIXED MINDSET**

Develops IQ and EI.

Sees intelligence and talent being developed over time.

BELIEFS

Sees intelligence and talent as fixed.

Sees IQ and EI as innate.

Motivated.

Persists in the face of setbacks. Motivated by challenges.

Challenges

Avoids challenges Feels threatened by challenges. Gives up easily.

Resistant.

Puts in more effort.

Believes that effort is important and leads to growth and mastery.

Effort

Believes that talent is innate so practice and effort are useless and not important.

Shows inertia.

Errors are lessons to be learned.

Views failures as temporary setback, learns, and persists.

Errors

Becomes demotivated, gives up easily, and views temporary setbacks as permanent failures.

Errors are failures; hides flaws.

Is inspired.

Sees other people's success as a source of inspiration.

Success of others

Sees other people's success as a source of threat or jealousy.

Compares.

Applies feedback.

Views feedback as an opportunity to grow, learns from and applies constructive criticism.

Feedback

Views feedback as personal and ignores constructive criticism.

Rejects criticism.

Develops competencies. Performs better than before. Embraces flaws and mistakes to learn.

FOCUS

Demonstrates competencies. Performs better than others. Hides flaws and mistakes to not feel ashamed.

Figure IV.2 Growth and fixed mindsets

People with a growth mindset have a passionate desire to achieve their goals and understand that this improvement process may be uncomfortable. People with a fixed mindset are more "closed-minded," with little space for growth.

Carol Dweck sums this up with the following statement [2]:

my research has shown that the view you adopt for yourself pro-
foundly affects the way you lead your life... Believing that your
qualities are carved in stone—the fixed mindset—creates an
urgency to prove yourself over and over. If you have only a certain
amount of intelligence, a certain personality, and a certain moral
character—well, then you'd better prove that you have a healthy
dose of them.

While more research is needed to clarify the precise brain activity of
people with growth mindsets, neuroimaging research has shown a link
between these mindsets and positive behaviors [35].

People with growth mindsets show a lower activation to negative feedback and higher activation in areas of the brain associated with higher
motivation, when learning, correcting errors, and adapting behaviors,
among others.

Carol Dweck's research has also pointed to the benefits of praising
the effort and resilience related to the process of growth, as opposed to
praising talent or natural abilities [36].

In "growth-minded people," the brain is most active when they were
told how they could improve, while for people with a fixed mindset, the
brain is active when they are being given information about their performance [37].

It is also important to understand that growth and fixed mindsets are
not a rigid dichotomy of operating in the world. One does not switch
between mindsets; rather, these exist on a continuum.

As Carol Dweck states,

Nobody has a growth mindset in everything all the time. Everyone is a mixture of fixed and growth mindsets. You could have
a predominant growth mindset in an area, but there can still be
things that trigger you into a fixed mindset trait.

In short, a growth mindset is not an end-state. It is an ongoing journey that starts with a realization about your current circumstances and
the potential opportunities that you have to grow. This journey involves

small, progressive shifts in thinking and behavior, as you create and change your habits.

Your goal is to understand this concept, to expand your growth mindset, and be able to recognize the fixed mindset triggers in yourself. This will allow you to identify obstacles as you take on challenges, embrace effort, and learn from your mistakes, as you work to create habits to achieve your goals.

***

🚀 Mission 13: Are You Growth or Fixed Mindset?

The following questions in Table IV.1 will help you understand where you are along the continuum between a fixed and growth mindset in relation to creating habits. Complete the table provided in the workbook.

Table IV.1 Fixed and growth mindset characteristics

	Fixed Mindset	**Growth Mindset**
Effort		
How do you view the effort required to achieve goals? Does it feel you are making progress or not?	"I won't put effort into this, as I'm not sure if I will succeed."	"I'm going to put in the effort to achieve my goal. I'm not sure when I will reach it, but I am going to try."
Challenges/obstacles		
How do you respond to challenges and obstacles?	"This problem appears to be impossible to solve. It looks like it won't work."	"I know that challenges are part of the process toward achieving my goals."
Errors		
Are you willing to try and fail?	"I don't want to look inept. I will only try this when I'm sure I can do it."	"I know mistakes are part of the process. I will keep trying until I get better."
Feedback		
What is your typical response to feedback, and how well do you accept it?	"Why are they criticizing my work?"	"I understand that everyone has different perspectives. Their points of view may be helpful."
Success of others		
Do you see other people's success as a threat or as evidence that your success may be achievable?	"She's done an amazing job. I doubt I could ever be as successful."	"I need to ask her how she did it and do something similar."

***

As the scientist, you have now successfully completed three voyages and executed a further seven missions! Key takeaways are:

- During your **second voyage**, *From the Amazon Rainforest to Europe*, you flew from the Amazon rainforest to southern Europe. You understood that **you can mobilize your thoughts, practice new ways of thinking, and reshape the communication between your neurons,** so that your brain circuits will become strengthened as you create habits.

- During your **third voyage**, *Friends or Foes*, you explored your brain systems and now understand that **you will need to create an optimum level of equilibrium between these systems.** This will **allow you to reflect**, ponder different options, weigh the short term versus the long term, and **take a more strategic approach to creating habits**.

- In your **10th voyage** *Identity System—Illusions and Mindsets*, you comprehended that **when you attempt to create habits, your *Identity System Illusion* and *Identity System Mindset* may be at play**. Realizing this will help you better understand the efforts you spend on protecting your core values and beliefs.

To devise habits, you need to know where your biases and other brain traps lie and adjust accordingly. On the other extreme, always recall that your brain remains "plastic" throughout a greater part of your life and that your potential to learn and grow is significant.

Armed with this knowledge, you are now ready for the next stage of your quest.

PART 3

The Painter

An artist who will paint self-portraits, both of current and desired states of identities, behaviors, and habits.

Everything you have read tells you that the inner workings of your brain systems, the psychological illusion of your *Identity System*, and your perceived mindset traits carve deep neural habit pathways in your brain infrastructure.

From how you educate your children, do business, manage your emotions, to interacting with colleagues and friends, these are habit pathways that drive your behavior over days, weeks, months, and years.

It is these same neural pathways that may unconsciously lead you to protect your *Identity System*. You paint what you believe are clear images of your past and can only create hazy sketches of your future. You have become an unreliable storyteller in the history you have created and are creating.

You project your self-image and view your environment zooming in and out through a lens based on subjective interpretations of your *Identity System*. Confined within predefined perimeters, you take decisions and actions that are neither in your self-interest nor in the interest of those around you.

In varying degrees, we all fall prey to these traps. This impairs our ability to identify and take on valuable opportunities and challenges for personal growth.

As William James told us,

All our life, so far as it has definite form, is but a mass of habits—practical, emotional and intellectual—systematically organized for our weal or woe and bearing us irresistibly toward our destiny, whatever the latter may be [38].

But what if instead of being irresistibly drawn to your destiny, you could plot your own North and systematically design the roads you wish to travel?

As the painter (see Figure 3.1), you will begin to choose and design your habits by looking at the long-term change you want to achieve—to improve your health, your work, and your life.

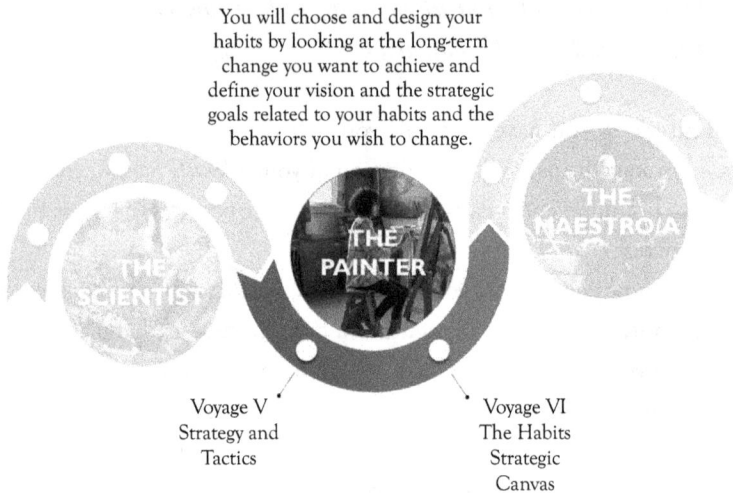

You will choose and design your habits by looking at the long-term change you want to achieve and define your vision and the strategic goals related to your habits and the behaviors you wish to change.

THE PAINTER

THE SCIENTIST

THE MAESTRO/A

Voyage V
Strategy and
Tactics

Voyage VI
The Habits
Strategic
Canvas

Figure 3.1 The long-term change

By defining your vision and the strategic goals related to your habits and the behaviors you wish to change, you will begin to intentionally harness the neuroplasticity of your brain, maximizing its performance across diverse and unfamiliar tasks.

Ready to take on this challenge? It is now time to assume your painter avatar and start your next voyage.

VOYAGE V

Strategy and Tactics

Victorious warriors win, then go to war; defeated warriors go to war and attempt to win.

—Sun Tzu

As the painter, you will be initially tasked with two **objectives for this voyage**. You need to:

⌖ Understand that it is **imperative to align your long-term focus with your short-term actions**.

⌖ Get an initial **grasp of the strategic–tactical voyages you will undertake** based on the Warp Speed Habits roadmap.

***

To achieve these objectives, you will execute one mission:

🚀 Mission 14: Think Strategically, Act Tactically
You should also review the Warp Speed Habits roadmap provided at the end of this voyage. This roadmap describes the various strategic–tactical voyages you will undertake.

***

Although your reflex to protect your *Identity System* never leaves you, you can leverage the unlimited potential of your brain's neuroplasticity to learn and grow. It is through your mental activity that you can become the sculptor of your brain infrastructure!

By intentionally defining and creating a development path that will enhance your performance, ultimately benefiting your teams and the organization you work for, you can enhance your current habits and build new ones.

It is this self-directed strategic approach that will allow you to begin to build new synaptic connections and strengthen existing synapses. This is a significant challenge that will truly require thinking differently.

Where to even begin?

Normally, you would ask yourself the question, "How do I motivate myself to act in a certain way?" A better question is, "Which process do I follow to create a habit, to leverage myself continuously to new thresholds of excellence?"

You will need to completely revamp your current approach to how you design, learn, and form habits. This will allow you to develop brain functions that you currently underutilize, as you transition from new to habitual behavior through the Habit Formation Matrix.

To explore this approach further, you will need to undertake two voyages and different missions.

In these voyages, you can be the Pablo Picasso (one of the most influential artists of the 20th century) or the Frida Kahlo (undoubtedly one of the most famous modern artists and perhaps the most renowned female painter), or any other painter of your choice, of designing habits.

This is a critical role, as in this voyage, you will understand the global strategic–tactical underpinnings needed to build habits and achieve successful individual change.

Reframe Your Approach

Approximately 2,500 years ago, Sun Tzu, considered as one of the greatest military strategists, stated that, "Strategy without tactics is the slowest route to victory. Tactics without strategy is the noise before defeat."[1]

What is most interesting in this quote is the clear interplay between strategy and tactics. Strategy that does not consider tactical specificities is ill-fated, and great tactics without strategy produces misalignment and incoherence. Unfortunately, this dialogue happens too rarely at an individual level.

---

[1] From *The Art of War*, a book that has influenced not only military thinking, but business tactics, legal strategy, lifestyles, and beyond.

From this starting point, the *Warp Speed Habits* model leverages a strategic–tactical business logic approach, incorporating neuroscience insights and lessons for creating habits.

In your journey toward your future *Identity System*, **the long-term focus of your strategy needs to be aligned with the short-term actions of your tactics** (see Figure V.1).

- Strategy is the "thinking," defining your long-term goals and the general path toward achieving your vision—this is your why.
- Tactics is the "acting," implementing more specific smaller actions with shorter timelines—this is your how.

Figure V.1 Strategy and tactics

***

🚀 Mission 14: Think Strategically, Act Tactically

In the following intuitive short exercise, classify the nature of the items as strategic or tactical. The answers to this mission are provided in the workbook.

- "Narrow" objectives, allowing for more focus: _____
- Represents the "why," your future *Identity System*: _____
- Includes short-term goals, three to six months out: _____

- Explains the "how": _____
- Stable and should not change in this period: _____
- Broad goals: _____
- Adjustable and can be changed quickly: _____
- Long term, six months to two years: _____

***

What Makes a Good Solid Strategy?

Your strategy is a formal summary of your aims and values. The result, a reflection of your future *Identity System*, is the foundation for all activities completed within the subsequent tactical cycle.

Critical activities you need to execute in the strategic cycle include **internal reflection, vision definition, and strategic goal setting**. The proficiency with which you **build your strategy** will guide your short-term choices and decision making as you work to achieve your strategic goals.

Your strategic planning process should be thorough, as you should only adjust your strategies in the long term, either as you grow or as new internal or external factors surface.

What Makes Great Tactics?

Your tactics will have clear objectives (subgoals) that need to be aligned with your strategic goals. Your tactics will have a short-term timeline, during which you complete specific activities and measure their outcomes.

The tactics you define will change over time, as your strategy becomes alive. It is also easier to adjust your tactics if these do not achieve the desired result than it is to rethink and rebuild your strategy.

Moving From Strategy to Tactics

You move from strategy to tactics within the strategy–tactics intersection (see Figure V.2). In this space, you will define your rules of tactical engagement and the metrics of your success. In the former, you will break down your strategy to tactics. In the latter, you measure your strategic and tactical outcomes.

Figure V.2 Strategy–tactics intersection

Through this integrated approach, you will understand, learn, and practice the science of habit creation in a structured, strategic–tactical, and brain-friendly manner.

Once you have mastered a habit by internalizing the skill within the tactical cycle and measured your success in the strategy–tactics intersection, you can return to the strategic cycle to review or define your next strategic challenge.

Strategic–Tactical Roadmap

The global roadmap of your strategic–tactical quest you will undertake using the *Habits Strategic Canvas* and the *Habits Tactical Sheet* is shown in Figure V.3.

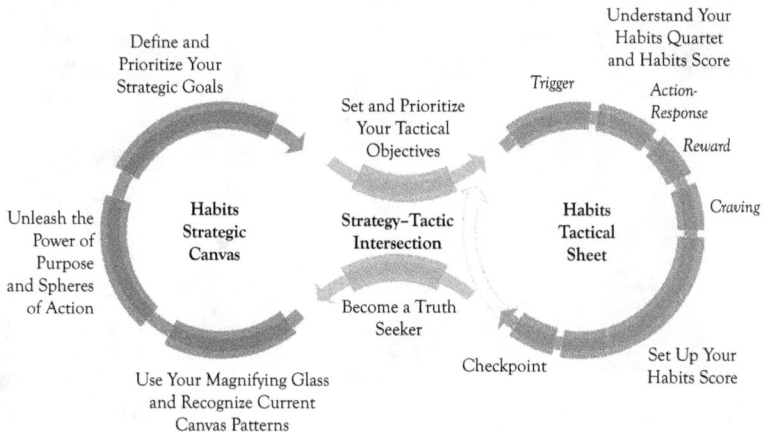

Figure V.3 Warp Speed Habits roadmap

During your voyages, you can refer to this roadmap to recap where you are in your quest.

You have now successfully completed your first important voyage as a painter. The mission you executed will have shown you that:

- **Aligning your tactics with your strategy is paramount**, as your vision will clearly guide your short-term choices and decision making.
- The **Warp Speed Habits roadmap provides a clear pathway** for the definition of both your strategy and your tactics, with a fundamental intersection between these.

VOYAGE VI

The Habits Strategic Canvas

Sound strategy starts with having the right goal.

—Michael Porter

During your third voyage *Friends or Foes*, you saw that your evolutionary "older" brain systems will override the more "younger systems." The latter will tire with too much effort. The former will favor the quick, necessary, and energy-efficient actions ensuring transitory survival.

As you traveled along the fourth voyage *Identity System: Illusion and Mindsets*, you also understood that your perception of your *Identity System* is not necessarily an accurate reflection of your history and experiences. Rather, your self-portrait may be a product of hazy and questionable interwoven narratives of your autobiographical memories.

With these observations in mind, your **objectives for this voyage** are:

◎ **Paint your current self-portrait** using the Habits Strategic Canvas. This canvas will allow you to **enhance your self-awareness and identify areas for improvement** in competencies you wish to grow.

◎ **Paint your future *Identity System*** and **appreciate its new narrative content.**

***

To achieve these objectives, you will need to execute eight missions:

🚀 Mission 15: Use Your Magnifying Glass
🚀 Mission 16: Recognize Current Canvas Patterns
🚀 Mission 17: Leverage Your Spheres of Action
🚀 Mission 18: Unleash the Power of Purpose
🚀 Mission 19: Define Your Strategic Goals
🚀 Mission 20: Rate Your Strategic Goals

🚀 Mission 21: Define Your Emotional Drivers
🚀 Mission 22: Prioritize Your Goals

***

A brief reminder before you move on. Much like Frida Kahlo with her brilliantly colored and uncompromising self-portraits, you need to remind yourself that your *Identity System* is orientative and adaptable rather than factual. This may prove challenging, as your brain will try to trap you, constantly drawing you back into your comfort zones and leading you to stumble.

Before you continue, it is time to meet Michael, your buddy during this journey. He will share his outputs with you as he works on his quest.

Meet Michael[1]

Michael is a program coordinator, recently promoted from the position of project manager, and is now responsible for leading six team leaders.

He is excited about the challenge, but apprehensive about leading his former peers. How will he motivate and engage them, how will he encourage "toward" states and avoid "away" states[2] in his team leaders?

Michael recognizes he performed well in his prior management role, but to get his team leaders and their teams to become high performing, to transform their organization, he realizes he needs to acquire new habits.

Fortunately for us, Michael has taken part in *Warp Speed Habits* training and is eager to share this knowledge.

As you venture through your voyages and missions, Michael will share with you his experiences as he completes his *Habits Strategic Canvas* and *Habits Tactical Sheet* and develops habits.

---

[1] Michael is a "combination" of different leaders and managers I have worked with and mentored.

[2] Neuroscientists describe the brain as having two functional states, *Toward* and *Away* states. When you feel a toward emotion, you will see more options, choices, and opportunities and can take in more information. When you are in an away state, your options, choices, and opportunities shrink and you take in less information! In the latter state, it is harder to create new habits!

Paint Your Current Self-Portrait

A fundamental basis of your quest includes your analysis and appreciation of the narrative content of the self-portrait you will paint using the *Habits Strategic Canvas* (see Figure VI.1).

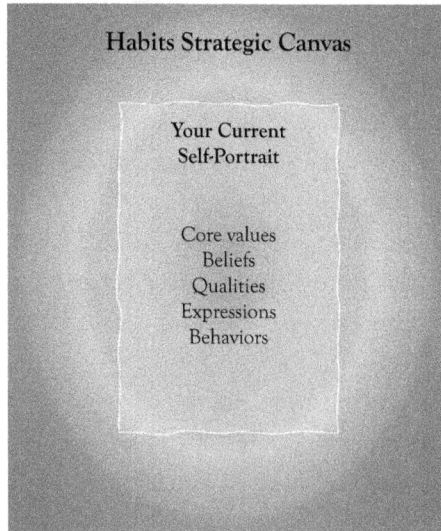

Figure VI.1 Habits Strategic Canvas

To understand the current neural pathways of your self-portrait, you will use a "self-reflection magnifying glass." This will allow you to become more self-aware and conscious of the broader details of your current *Identity System*, including your core values, passions, aspirations, thoughts, feelings, and expressions.

This reflection will enhance your perception of how your *Identity System* plays out in your social, emotional, and (ir)rational interactions in response to events and stimuli. You will be able to identify gaps and opportunities for improvement, potential areas where you can apply more colors, intensity, and depth to your canvas.

Be forewarned that although your brain is equipped for self-awareness, you (and most of the human population) are not good at it.

In a five-year research program on this subject, findings show that although a **whopping 95 percent of people think they're self-aware, only 10 to 15 percent are** [39]!

And if you are in a leadership position, then you will need to be doubly cautious, as you are more likely to overestimate your capabilities in this domain [40].

Why is this capability so underdeveloped?

- This may be an exercise that you do not execute often and hence your self-reflection neural pathways are not consolidated.
- You may find this exercise difficult, as you will question your *Identity System* and the way you implicitly define yourself in your role.
- When in a leadership position, the potential for self-awareness may be overshadowed by self-centered behaviors of perceived power, dominance of knowledge, and feedback avoidance [41].

Benjamin Franklin[3] hit it on the nail in the 1750 edition of Poor Richard's Almanack when he wrote, **"There are three things extremely hard, steel, a diamond and to know oneself."**

***

🚀 Mission 15: Use Your Magnifying Glass

If you cannot reflect on your current self-portrait, you will have no basis for taking on new challenges. You will not be able to monitor the intensity, color, dimensions, and depth of your self-portrait and identify potential improvements.

Self-awareness is a capability difficult to develop, but fundamental for those who want to build or change habits. Ask yourself the following questions:

- Do you find yourself not listening to others?
- Do you have difficulty accepting feedback?

---

[3] Benjamin Franklin was an American printer and publisher, author, inventor, scientist, and diplomat. One of the foremost of the Founding Fathers, Franklin helped draft the Declaration of Independence.

- Do you have difficulty understanding other people's perspectives?
- Do you have difficulty in "reading between the lines" when you walk into a room and tailoring your message to your audience?
- Do you have an inflated opinion of yourself and your performance?

  If you've replied positively to any of these questions, you may still think that you are self-aware, but are probably not. You are demonstrating behaviors consistent with individuals that are not self-aware [42].

***

To start developing the capability of self-awareness, you need to commit to doing tough introspection. This is a habit you will need to develop and use to:

- Understand what potentially keeps you from committing to new habits.
- Understand your current versus past performance.
- Develop an instinctive sense of the color, depth, and outer limits of your self-portrait on your canvas.
- Create habits with a focus on long-term improvement.

With increasing self-awareness comes an ability enabling you to take on challenges. You will be able to apply more color and intensity to your self-portrait and stretch your canvas continuously. You will draw uncompromising sketches of your behavioral adjustments and paint brilliantly colored future self-portraits.

How can you enhance this much-needed capability of developmental self-awareness? How can you begin to see the assumptions, biases, and other blemishes that you may be blind to, in the canvas of your current self-portrait? How can you see and understand the patterns, series of opportunities, shifts, and brush strokes you will need to apply to your painting?

***

🚀 Mission 16: Recognize Current Canvas Patterns

To paint your self-portrait, you will carry out several exercises to help stimulate your self-awareness capability, or metacognition, as psychologists and neuroscientists call it [43].

As explained by Stephen Fleming, author of *Know Thyself: The Science of Self-Awareness,* metacognition is "our mind's ability to reflect on, think about, and know things about itself, including how it remembers, perceives, decides, thinks, and feels." It is your ability to think about your own thinking.

To carry out this mission, you will need to set aside a couple of hourly sessions. Before you start, find a quiet and safe place to sit, with no distractions, to leverage your focus. This is an essential part of painting your self-portrait.

You can keep the sketch simple as you start. Over time, you can add more complexity. Allow yourself to adjust as brain traps and your *Identity System Illusion and Mindset* attempt to impede your passage, but above all, dedicate yourself to the process.

As you go through the six exercises shown in Figure VI.2, you will develop an awareness of the self, your wants, needs, desires, and your strengths and weaknesses, allowing you to connect with your *Identity System.*

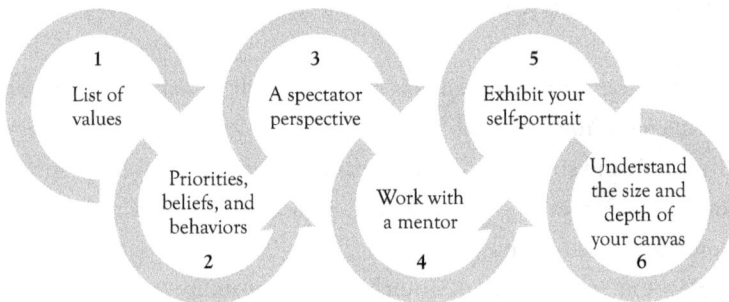

1	3	5
List of values	A spectator perspective	Exhibit your self-portrait
Priorities, beliefs, and behaviors	Work with a mentor	Understand the size and depth of your canvas
2	4	6

Figure VI.2 Recognizing canvas patterns

1. Create a List of Values

You can do the following 15-to-20-minute exercise individually or with a colleague, as you document the findings in your workbook.

You will create a preliminary self-portrait on your canvas, to help you understand your values. You should try to complete the first version in one session.

List two to three aspects that you value most in the categories shown in Table VI.1, at the same time providing a brief description of what these mean to you.

Table VI.1 List and description of values

		Values					
		1	Description	2	Description	3	Description
Categories	Yourself						
	Leaders						
	Team members						
	Peers						
	Organizational culture						

As you consider the categories listed and to facilitate this exercise, ask yourself the following questions:

- Can you identify five to six of your most important values? Think of aspects such as trust and integrity, and their meaning to you.
- Think of your strengths that other people have referred to. How have these leveraged your accomplishments?
- What other strengths do you consider you have?
- What do you believe are your weaknesses, and how do these affect your performance?
- Have other people commented on your weaknesses?
- Can you identify the drivers in your work environment or culture that make you feel engaged, excited, and an active contributor?
- What skills do you bring to your workplace that you underutilize?
- What are the major characteristics of the leaders and co-workers in your organization?

Once you have completed this exercise, reflect on how it went. Was it easy or more challenging than you expected? You will be surprised to learn that many people cannot articulate their values clearly the first time round.

You have now captured your general perception of:

- Values in your work environment that you consider are important
- The composition and description of these values
- How you see and project yourself

It does not have to be an exact painting. As you come back over time to this exercise, you will add, reprioritize, or adjust some values captured, and identify flawed biases.

Michael's List and Description of Values

Michael found this first exercise quite challenging, but after getting started, he gathered momentum.

His output for this first exercise appears in Figure VI.3.

In the following exercises in this mission, you will add intensity, a variety of colors, varying brush strokes, and further details to your painting.

2. Reflect Upon Priorities, Beliefs, and Behaviors

In this exercise, you will understand why the values you described are important, how they affect your current actions, and how they will affect your future actions within your work environment.

Your answers to the probing questions mentioned later, categorized into priorities, beliefs, and behaviors (see Figure VI.4), will give you an increasing awareness of the values associated with your self-portrait and the way you interact with and are perceived by your world.

As a result of this exercise, you may leave some values untouched on your canvas, but will make others richer, more complex, and denser.

Categories	Aspects					
	1	Description	2	Description	3	Description
Yourself	Positive attitude	Positive social interactions; managing emotions; seeing bright side of challenges	Fairness	Improve inclinations toward colleagues; eliminate/reduce biases	Self-esteem	Candidly appreciate and like myself regardless of the circumstances
Leaders	Integrity	Strong moral principles	Trustworthy	Deserving of trust	Visionary	Long-term thinking
Team members	Integrated	Excel at working together/teamwork	Positive mindset	Openness to learn from others; Curious; Determination to grow	Ambition	Work to achieve stretch targets
Colleagues	Positive peer group	Inspire positive choices; support others	Diversity	Bring in diverse perspectives and assure inclusion	Respect	Treat others with respect
Organizational culture	Continuous improvement	Continuously challenge the status quo	Collaborative environment	Work together to achieve more	Equity	Diversity and inclusion

Figure VI.3 Michael's list and description of values

Figure VI.4 Priorities, beliefs, and behaviors

Priorities

- Which values appear the most in the distinct categories?
- Do you consider these values to be important?
- Why are these values across the various categories important to you?

Beliefs

- Why do you do what you do and believe what you believe?
- Do you know the sources of your values?
- How did you come to hold these values?
- Were these values present in your childhood or adulthood?
- Do these core values and principles originate from an internal or external source of status and authority?

Behaviors

- Which of these values relate to activities that you carried out today or yesterday?
- If you keep carrying out these activities, where will you be in two, five, or 10 years from now?
- How do you think the aspects listed for yourself affect your behavior toward others?
- How do you think that the behavioral aspects you listed in the categories related to leaders, team members, and colleagues impact behavior in yourself and others, and what is the overall impact on the organizational culture?

Shortlist Your Values

Based on your reflection, select two values that you feel you need to improve and that you can leverage to augment your *Identity System*.

With this current *Identity System* reflection and the areas of improvement opportunities selected, you will gain an awareness that will open you up to new possibilities, allowing you to apply different brush strokes and colors to your portrait, and extend the outer limits of your canvas.

You will still "respect" your *Identity System*; you will just begin to "loosen" your attachment to your current *Identity System* frame of mind.

Michael's Reflection and Shortlist of Opportunities

From his reflection, Michael has selected two values he feels affect his behavior in the work environment.

1. Positive Attitude

Michael has seen that certain events at work have an emotional impact on his colleagues and peers, with the consequent emotional states affecting both behaviors and attitudes.

From critical and unconstructive feedback after weeks of challenging work, to when a customer or colleague snaps at him, to when his boss assigns him more work, leading to more overload, these or similar events have contributed to anger, frustration, irritation, disappointment, or unhappiness.

Michael has seen how these emotions in himself, and others, can lead to an unproductive workplace.

He also recognizes that managing and regulating his emotions in potentially conflictual social encounters is critical to creating positive functional environments.

2. Fairness

Michael feels that unfair dispositions and biases are prevalent in his behaviors, as well as among some of his peers and team members, leading to an uncomfortable compromise for the sake of social cohesion.

Following this reflection, he now knows that he will need to challenge and overcome these behavioral biases.

---

3. Become a Spectator of Your Self-Portrait

Now that you've added contrast to your self-portrait, you can give it even more depth, color, and intensity by taking a spectator perspective of the painting on your canvas and the areas you want to enhance.

Imagine walking into your private art gallery and seeing your collection, with your self-portrait that you've commissioned and painted yourself.

Ask yourself:

- Do you recall situations where your values were starkly present and made you or other people feel uncomfortable?
- What could be wrong in the painting, in your values and behaviors?
- Can there be other ways of seeing the world apart from your perspective, just as true as the brush strokes on your self-portrait?
- Based on your replies, are you able to identify assumptions, biases, and other blemishes that are present in your self-portrait?

This learning perspective of introspection, consistently applied to every bit of your self-portrait, is tough. Much like learning to mix colors to get the tone right, by asking yourself these questions, you recognize that other people's perspectives can be just as true as your own.

During this process, write what you are thinking and the emotions you are feeling, making your thoughts and thought processes more tangible.

Initially, you will have to force yourself to think constantly about the answers to these questions, and you will need to have the patience to check your perspective as your self-portrait progresses.

Over time and with practice, this reflection process will become increasingly instinctive as you will learn to create internal psychological flexibility and open yourself up to new possibilities.

As you evaluate your self-portrait courageously and candidly, you will recognize your ego and self-importance, errors, and mistakes, and move beyond the density and perimeters of a potentially subjective self-portrait.

Michael's Spectator Perspective

It took some time for Michael to adjust to this exercise but working with a mentor (see step *4. Work With a Mentor*) who constantly challenged his perceptions, he was able to become a spectator of his self-portrait, gradually distancing himself and analyzing it from a third-person perspective.

From the two areas chosen, he was able to provide more depth to his initial brush strokes.

1. Positive Attitude

Michael recognized that in certain situations, his direct and instinctive responses, which seemed correct at the time, had led to uncomfortable away states from his team leaders and colleagues.

Michael acknowledged that managing and regulating his emotions, in potentially conflictual social encounters, was critical to creating positive functional environments.

2. Fairness

Reflecting upon certain events, he realized that several behavioral biases in the organization had blinded him and others and generated unfair situations, with a detrimental impact on individual performance and team dynamics.

Following this reflection, he now knows that he will need to challenge and overcome these behavioral biases.

4. Work With a Mentor

Working with a mentor is the same as inviting a highly regarded experienced art critic to work with you in analyzing your private art collection.

As you interact with your "art critic," you will ask for and get direct and objective feedback about your areas of opportunity.

This trusted adviser should provide positive reinforcement and challenge your perceptions and knowledge to help grow your confidence levels and performance.

Your mentor should work with you to track your progress, identify small ways for you to improve, and hold you accountable to deliver your best effort each day, as you tackle your areas of opportunity.

Working with a mentor not only requires time, effort, and sustained deliberate practice but requires you to be open-minded and to trust your mentor's "critique."

5. Exhibit Your Self-Portrait

Exhibiting your self-portrait is about observing how people around you respond to your self-portrait as your behavioral values are playing out [44].

This act requires heightened self-awareness, as you are exhibiting your private art collection (your self-portrait) to people you interact with and seeing how they react in real-time, without them being aware of this.

This is a challenging task, as you need to be present in the moment and focused on the conversation at hand. As you view how people acknowledge the brush strokes on your painting, ask yourself how they are responding. Look at their facial expressions and body language. Are they tense or relaxed, engaged in a half-hearted conversation, or concentrated and listening? Are they formal, or informal, critical, or accepting of your self-portrait?

Michael's Exhibition of His Self-Portrait

Just like Michael, as you attempt to implement this exercise, you will see that it is a major challenge, as you sway between two distinct roles, that of the observer and that of the participant.

This specific exercise will take time, patience, and significant practice to integrate the roles of observer and participant.

6. Understand the Size and Depth of Your Self-Portrait and Canvas

This mission in your quest will require time, practice, willingness, and above all humility, as you discover and examine your core values, beliefs, and principles that govern your *Identity System*.

Recap on the results of the exercises you carried out as you completed and critiqued your self-portrait and identified areas of opportunity for growth.

You will realize that it represents a tipping point between the potential benefits of creating habits and the associated threats that these changes will inevitably bring about.

You may find yourself feeling some discomfort, uneasiness, and perhaps confusion, as your self-awareness increases, and your unconscious brain attempts to limit the perimeters and depth of the self-portrait on your canvas (see Figure VI.5).

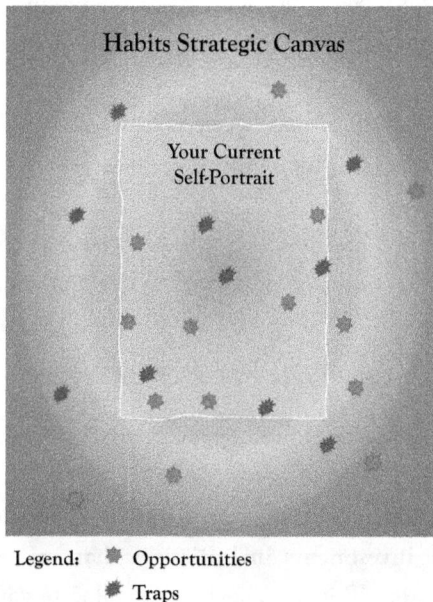

Figure VI.5 Current self-portrait—opportunities and traps

You have potentially reached the limits of the amount and type of risk you are prepared to pursue or tolerate.

***

As you progress in your quest and develop an intuitive sense of the depth, perimeters, and comfort zones of your self-portrait on your canvas, you will see that these will change in size, as you implement significant changes and identify further areas of developmental opportunities.

Above all, you will understand that to create habits consistently and effectively, it is fundamental that you build this self-reflection capability.

This periodic reflection, which sits within the strategic cycle, should occur once every three to six months. In your painter role, you will assess your unfinished artwork to understand its three-dimensional depth and the intensity of its textures and colors, before adding complexity or simplicity to your never-ending masterpiece.

Outline Your Future Self-Portrait

In the prior missions, you understood and validated the internal intrinsic qualities and personal characteristics that you are proud of. You now also have a good notion of the values that you would like to improve as well as the behaviors that support these values.

Now, applying business management logic, you will delve into the areas of opportunities of your self-portrait and subsequently define your vision.

In the first of two missions, you will detail areas of opportunities on the self-portrait of your canvas using spheres of action (SoA).

Define Your Spheres of Action

Think of SoA[4] as areas of similar opportunities within or next to your self-portrait on your current canvas.

By targeting and actioning your areas of opportunities in SoA, you will ensure investments in initiatives that are crucial to your long-term strategies. This will allow you to allocate your time, effort, energy, and knowledge to the behaviors and habits you need to focus on.

These SoA will help extend the boundaries of your self-portrait or give more depth to the painting on your canvas, by defining new areas for learning and growth. These are areas where you will apply defter brush strokes to parts of the portrait you need to improve or where you will pencil outlines of images that you wish to create.

---

[4] Global Innovation Management Institute (GIMI) deserves special recognition for their influence on this concept. The SoA applied at an individual level is loosely based on the concept of fields of play applied at a business innovation level.

THE HABITS STRATEGIC CANVAS   81

A critical aspect to consider is the SoA you will choose.

You will recall from your fourth voyage *Identity System—Illusions and Mindsets* that your reflex to protect your *Identity System* will never leave you. It is therefore important to understand that a habit that you want to create will hold greater (subjective) value to the degree that it relates to your *Identity System*.

Selecting SoA that allow you to keep important aspects of your Identity System will allow you to have at least one foot within your current self-portrait. These SoA should be highly actionable as they still tap into your major strengths, albeit the extreme limits of your capabilities. This will allow you to take on challenges that are just beyond the outer limits of your reach (see Figure VI.6).

This does not mean you should not select audacious SoA that are more distant from your current self-portrait. You just need to know that by doing this, you are increasing the difficulty of the challenge you will face in creating habits.

By allowing you to keep important aspects of your *Identity System*, these SoA go hand-in-hand with developing a habits growth mindset.

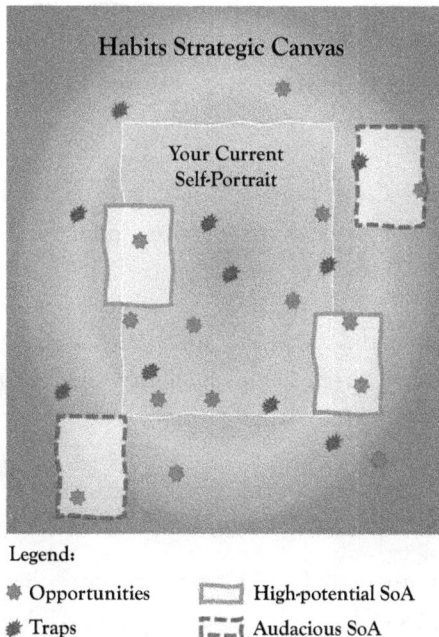

Figure VI.6 Spheres of action (SoA)

This will leverage and inspire you to learn, take healthy risks to expand the possible, and increase your psychological flexibility. This will also facilitate the creation of new and solid neural pathways, leading to positive outcomes for the SoA you have chosen.

You can assimilate SoA to keystone habits, a concept popularized by Charles Duhigg in his book *The Power of Habit*. He recognizes that specific habits have the power to transform other behaviors without paying attention to those areas.

For example, leaders who have developed SoA of managing their emotions and creating a positive emotional climate improve rapport in their teams and create perceived equity in the work environment, leading to improved team performance [45].

By focusing on key SoA, patterns in other areas shift and culture change becomes contagious.

To further understand the context of SoA, let's look at how Michael developed his.

Michael's SoA

Michael has identified two areas of opportunities, namely the need to create a positive functional work environment and to tackle biases in the workplace.

Based on these areas of opportunities, Michael has defined two SoA:

1. **Sentiment**—Create functional team environments.
2. **Bias**—Challenge and overcome social, emotional, and (ir)rational behavioral biases in the workplace.

Michael knows that these SoA are both challenging and actionable and will contribute to improving his leadership skills.

***

🚀 Mission 17: Leverage Your Spheres of Action

Based on your purpose and the example shown earlier, you can now define your SoA. Use the template provided in the workbook.

***

Vision Statements

Organizations use mission and vision statements to outline the purpose of their existence in the former and identify the destination point and the values that drive actions in the latter.

As an individual, you may already have a purpose for doing what you do, **personal goals** that lead you through work and life.

Formalizing these into tangible black-and-white vision statements is fundamental to providing the direction to chart the course of the choices you will make and the habits you wish to create.

Your vision statement has obvious benefits, as it:

1. Is *Identity System* **directed**, with vital information about your future self, summarized into a few sentences.
2. Allows for **long-term focus** and thinking and gives you purpose and motivation to keep going. You should craft a vision statement for one to three years.
3. Provides **clarity on the why and what of your actions**, directing you to specific questions that orient your choices.
4. **Facilitates decision making**, serving as a reminder about what is important to you and what is not important!
5. **Holds you accountable** by creating a reviewable reinforcement of your purpose, helping to keep you on track.

***

🚀 Mission 18: Unleash the Power of Purpose

Set aside a couple of hours to work on your vision statement. At this stage, do not attempt to achieve an exact painting of your future self-portrait.

Over time, as you come back to this exercise, you may add to or adjust your vision as, for example, you review the priorities of your values or identify flaws and biases you wish to improve.

Use the template provided in the workbook. The steps required for you to craft your vision include the following steps.

Step 1—*Review Your Values*

Review the fundamental values you defined and the output of your self-awareness exercises from the prior missions. Once you have concluded this step, you are ready to design a personal vision statement.

Step 2—*Craft Your Vision*

Write in the first person and craft a vision that reflects the values and opportunities you have identified. Write the statements as if you are already making them happen, as this will help you see it in your mind's eye.

The first part of the statement should contain your purpose, while the second part should explain the "general how" you will achieve your purpose.

Your vision statement should communicate your purpose in approximately 50 to 100 words. It needs to be concise, powerful, and uplifting.

Step 3—*Review Your Vision*

When finished, review and read your completed statement out loud. Your purpose must be clear and inspire you to continue your quest.

Look at Michael's vision statement before drafting yours.

Michael's Vision Statement

Purpose

I am a source of stability and inspiration for my team leaders and teams.

General How

My actions promote harmony among my teams and increase everyone's chance for success. I persist after setbacks and focus on what I can do to improve my leadership skills and increase my value.

When stress threatens to overtake me, I consciously take time to calm down to prevent acting with annoyance or hostility toward others.

I also seek support from others. By listening to and serving others, I learn innovative ideas and gain different perspectives.

As you apply more texture and color to your self-portrait and move from one overlapping SoA to another, you will increase the dimensions and depth of your canvas and enhance your brain infrastructure.

It is, however, important to remember that your older ways of making sense of your world, your old neural maps, do not vanish but remain within you.

Brain traps may, unbidden, rear their heads now and again, knocking you off-balance, and you may find yourself making excuses, rationalizing your actions and behaviors, and illuding yourself.

But now you are not only armed with knowledge related to your *Final Frontier* and *Identity Systems Illusions and Mindsets*, but also understand the power of neuroplasticity and have clarity about your vision and SoA. Even if you get battered in the rough seas of life, you will be able to ride out these storms.

In your next mission, using the *Habits Strategic Canvas*, you will define your strategic goals linked to your vision and each of the SoA. How you do this is crucial for the successful pursuit of habit creation.

The Context of Strategic Goals

You will recall that your strategic goals will represent your "why," your future *Identity System*, essentially defining the global direction you will take to achieve your desired future state.

These are broad goals, usually long term in nature, six months to two years out. They should be stable and not change much during this period.

Think of these as the sweeping strokes, outlines, and colors you wish to apply to the SoA on your canvas.

Further into your quest, in your voyage *The Strategy–Tactic Intersection*, you will break down your strategic goals into tactical objectives or subgoals. The latter will be used to orient your *Habits Quartet*.

Now that you've understood the context of strategic goals, you can define these for the SoA you established in the prior mission. Once completed, you will assess and prioritize these. Before defining your strategic goals, look at Michael's preliminary strategic goals.

Michael's Strategic Goals

Michael has defined various strategic goals for his SoA.

SoA 1: Sentiment—Create functional team environments.

SoA 1: Strategic Goals

1. I will become emotionally self-aware and be able to read and understand my emotions, as well as their impact on relationships in the workplace.
2. I will achieve better self-control to improve my performance at work.

SoA 2: Bias—Challenge and overcome social, emotional, and (ir)rational behavioral biases in the workplace.

SoA 2: Strategic Goals

1. I will be more socially aware of other people's emotions, understand their perspectives, and take an active interest in their concerns.
2. I will smooth out disagreements, manage conflicts, and orchestrate resolutions.

***

🚀 Mission 19: Define Your Strategic Goals

You can now define your strategic goals. Use the template provided in the workbook to complete this mission. Once defined, you will be ready to assess and prioritize your goals.

***

Assess Your Strategic Goals

As you've seen from Michael's strategic goals and those you've defined, the **result of achieving your goals implies deviating from your current *Identity System*.**

As you want to give more depth to your self-portrait or increase the perimeter of your canvas, you will paint an image that will branch off from established neural pathways, and as you now know, creating neural pathways is difficult.

To enhance your possibilities of success, you will assess your goals, rating these against seven strategic goal criteria.

1. The first criterion to consider is the number of your strategic goals.
   You will then review each goal selected against the following criteria:
2. Alignment to your SoA.
3. Simple, clear, and easy to recall.
4. Emotionally relevant.
5. Effort you will put in.
6. Approach versus avoidance-oriented strategic goals.
7. Challenging, measurable, and time-bound strategic goals.

***

🚀 Mission 20: Rate Your Strategic Goals

You should now review each criterion for your strategic goals. Use your workbook to complete the rating of your goals. Where relevant, for each criterion, Michael's output will be provided.

1. **Are my strategic goals limited in number?**
   Your brain is a powerful organ, but as you've seen, you will need to consider your executive system's cognitive capacity and constraints.

   Too many choices vying for your attention is exhausting and paralyzing to your brain. You need to minimize the amount of information you process by focusing on two to three key goals that apply to your SoA.

   As stated by Peter Drucker, father of modern management, "the key to strategy is omission." This is corroborated in *The 4 Disciplines of Execution,*[5] where the first discipline is to narrow the focus on the wildly important.

This goes against our basic wiring, but **a reduction in the number of goals leads to more goals being achieved with excellence.** Rate this first criterion using the scale shown in Figure VI.7.

Are my strategic goals limited in number?									
1	2	3	4	5	6	7	8	9	10

1 = Too many objectives; 5 = Can reduce number; 10 = Just correct.

Figure VI.7 Number of strategic goals

Michael started with two SoA and four goals but reduced these to the first SoA (sentiment) and the **related two goals of emotional self-awareness and self-control.**

Now, for each of your strategic goals selected, review the following criteria.

2. **Is my strategic goal aligned to my SoA?**

In the prior mission, you selected SoA which allowed you to keep important aspects of your *Identity System.*

Your strategic goals will work best when they are relevant and aligned to your SoA—your commitment will be greater when you believe in what you are doing.

To ensure the alignment of your strategic goals to your SoA, you need to understand how meaningful your goals are. For this effect, rate the second criterion using the scale shown in Figure VI.8.

In Michael's case, these are goals of high importance, clearly aligned with his SoA and the *Identity System* that he wants to paint.

---

[5] The *4 Disciplines of Execution: Achieving Your Wildly Important Goals* is a book written by Stephen Covey, related to the creation of organizational change.

Is my strategic goal important to me? Does it provide meaning to my SoA?									
1	2	3	4	5	6	7	8	9	10
1 = Low importance; 5 = Moderate importance; 10 = High importance.									

Figure VI.8 Importance of strategic goal

3. Is my strategic goal simple, clear, and easy to recall?

Your limited number of goals **must be simple and take low cognitive effort to recall** [46], sticking like glue in your memory—what is memorable is more easily retrievable and acted upon [47].

For each goal selected, rate the third criterion using the scale shown in Figure VI.9.

Is my strategic goal simple, clear, and easy to recall?									
1	2	3	4	5	6	7	8	9	10
1 = Difficult to recall; 5 = Moderately easy to recall; 10 = Easy to recall.									

Figure VI.9 Memorable goals

After Michael reviewed his goals based on the criterion above, he simplified his goals to the following statements:

- I will understand my emotions and their impact on relationships.
- I will manage my emotions constructively to leverage performance.

4. Is my strategic goal emotionally relevant?

You can think of the emotional relevance of your goals as the fuel you will need to maintain your effort and persistence and to increase your odds of success, as you will face countless setbacks in creating habits.

Studies show that **emotionally significant goals cause participants to focus on goal achievement and downgrade the difficulty**

of achieving goals, avoiding behaviors that don't contribute to the goals [48, 49].

From a brain perspective, the degree to which the goal is emotionally relevant is evaluated by your risk analysis system. This relevance is leveraged by the frontal lobes of your executive system that defines the specifics of the goals and maintains representations of these in your working memory. Relevant goals are given precedence in the access of your selective attention [48].

Positive emotions such as joy and excitement, but emotions such as anger and frustration are also emotional drivers you will need to pursue your goals.

Do you know the emotional drivers that fuel your energy and if these are present in your goals?

Before continuing with mission 20, take a couple of minutes and use your workbook to review and define some of your emotional drivers.

***

🚀 Mission 21: Define Your Emotional Drivers

Look at the list of the positive and negative emotional drivers in Table VI.2. Select those or define others that are pertinent to your goals, completing the template provided in the workbook.

Table VI.2 Positive and negative drivers

Positive Drivers	Negative Drivers
Joyous	Angry
Excited	Frustrated
Valued	Vulnerable
Confident	Upset
Empowered	Manipulated
Inspired	Intimidated
Enthusiastic	Anxious
...	..

***

In Michael's case, he has implicit positive emotional drivers associated with his strategic goals, as shown in the phrases:

- "… understand… impact (of my emotions) on relationships."—This will give him the knowledge and confidence to understand his behaviors and their impact; and
- "… manage… emotions… to leverage performance." —This will make him feel inspired and empowered.

Once you have defined your emotional drivers, continue with mission 20 and rate the criterion, shown in Figure VI.10, to understand whether emotional drivers fuel your energy.

Do emotions drive my strategic goal?									
1	2	3	4	5	6	7	8	9	10

1 = Insignificant emotional drivers; 5 = Moderate emotional drivers; 10 = Intense emotional drivers.

Figure VI.10 Emotional relevance of strategic goals

5. **How much effort will I put in to achieve my strategic goal?**
   Effort is about your commitment and constant drive for achievement and demonstrates your desire and intent for wanting to achieve your strategic goals and priorities.

   Even if you have opted for a more challenging SoA, a firm belief in your capacity for achievement is essential. This confidence will have been or should be acquired by knowledge, practice, experience, and effort.

   How important is the new behavior? Are you determined and willing to put in effort? Rate this criterion using the scale shown in Figure VI.11.

How much effort will I put in to achieve my strategic goal?									
1	2	3	4	5	6	7	8	9	10

1 = Will not expend any effort; 5 = Will put in some effort; 10 = Will give it all I've got.

Figure VI.11 Strategic goals and effort you will put in

> In Michael's case, he knows he will deliver maximum effort to achieve
> his strategic goals—they are fundamental in his leadership role.

6. **Is my strategic goal approach oriented?**

   The way you think about and frame your goals in relation to your
   Identity System and your SoA is important.

   You can have a mindset that is approach or avoidance-based in
   relation to your strategic goals.

   With an approach mindset, you define and frame your goals to
   achieve and maintain a desirable outcome, for example, tackling
   conflict to create a functional environment.

   With an avoidance mindset, you define and frame your
   goals to avoid or eliminate an undesirable outcome, for example, avoiding conflict to minimize contributing to a dysfunctional
   environment.

   By framing your goals to your mindset, a study suggests that you
   will enhance your motivation and leverage your outcomes [50].

   Rate this criterion using the scale shown in Figure VI.12.

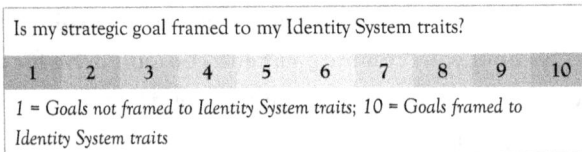

Is my strategic goal framed to my Identity System traits?									
1	2	3	4	5	6	7	8	9	10

*1 = Goals not framed to Identity System traits; 10 = Goals framed to
Identity System traits*

Figure VI.12 Identity system traits of strategic goals

Having said this, it is also important to consider that your emotions are at play in this approach-avoidance goal framework.

Research shows that striving toward a greater number of avoidance goals relates to [51]:

- Less pride and joy with progress
- Fewer positive feelings about progress with personal goals
- Reduced self-esteem, self-control, and vitality
- Low satisfaction with life
- Feeling less able to pursue goals

If you approach goal setting from an avoidance mindset, this may be an opportune time to adjust your mindset. You will become more positive and motivated to act on your intentions, inciting further action.

As you can see in Michael's goals, they are both approach oriented.

Rate this criterion using the scale shown in Figure VI.13.

Do I have an avoidance or approach mindset?

| 1 | 2 | 3 | 4 | 5 | 6 | 7 | 8 | 9 | 10 |

1 = Avoidance mindset; 10 = Approach mindset.

Figure VI.13 Strategic goals and mindset traits

7. **Is my strategic goal challenging, measurable, and time-bound?**
   One of the most consistent findings across diverse studies is that **challenging, stretch goals, pushing you just beyond your current self-portrait's comfort zone into your risk zone, where your *Identity System* requires more depth and consistency, lead to higher performance** than easily achievable goals [52, 53].

   But individuals generally have difficulty in defining stretch goals, as they commit themselves to goals that are highly desirable but less feasible when the future is distant and prefer goals that are less desirable but highly feasible in the near future [54].

   Challenging goals direct your attention, mobilize your effort, and increase your persistence, but how do you define the optimal amount of stretch?

   Recalling the inverted-U curve, a goal that has little to no stretch will not motivate you (see Figure VI.14).

   As you move toward the top of the curve, the stretch of the goal increases, as does the cognitive performance of your executive system. Pursuing these goals is exciting and seems almost effortless. This vibrant and focused toward state will persist through to the top of the curve.

   From this turning point onwards, doubt about the achievability of the goal will lead to a threat state. A goal that seems unreachable will also fail to motivate you, and your executive system will feel overwhelmed.

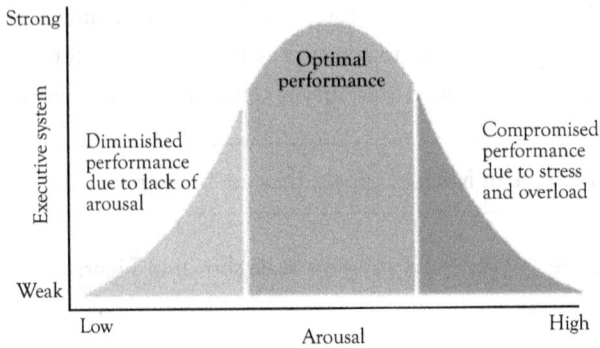

Figure VI.14 Inverted-U and stretch goals

What does this mean? When setting goals, you will need to create greater neural activation by ensuring a balance between the neurotransmitter's norepinephrine and dopamine (see Figure VI.15).

Make sure that your goals are sufficiently challenging and time-bound, pushing you to your limit, while allowing you to make enough progress to stay motivated and focused.

In relation to the measurability of your goals, at this stage, all that is required is your (subjective) appreciation of this aspect, as you

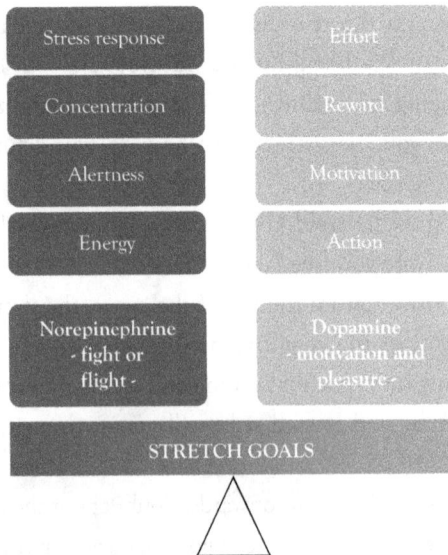

Figure VI.15 Stretch goals and balanced neurotransmitters

will tackle this point in some depth in *Voyage IX: Full Cycle—From Tactics to Strategy*, where you will define specific measures and targets for your strategic goals and tactical objectives.

Rate this criterion using the scale shown in Figure VI.16.

Is my strategic goal challenging, measurable, and time-bound?									
1	2	3	4	5	6	7	8	9	10

1 = Nonstretch objectives; 5 = Can incorporate more stretch;
10 = Stretch just right and measurable.

Figure VI.16 Challenging strategic goals

After Michael reviewed his goals based on the criterion aforementioned, he included stretch in his goals by qualifying the phrase and adding a timeline.

- Within six months, I will fully understand my emotions and their impact on relationships.
- Within six months, I will manage my emotions constructively to leverage performance.

***

🚀 Mission 22: Prioritize Your Goals

Now that you have assessed the criteria for your strategic goals, the next step is to determine your goal priorities. Prioritizing your goals will allow you to reduce your uncertainty, psychological costs, and cognitive load.

This is fundamental for several reasons:

- This will help you decide which strategic goal takes priority.
- To allocate your energy, talent, and the limited time you have to pursue your high-priority goals.
- To clarify how to handle conflicting goals with competing total scores.

Define your priorities at this stage. Review the average criteria score for each strategic goal in your workbook. If you have goals with competing total scores, define a second level of prioritization, for example, prioritizing the goals where you ranked highest on the effort and emotional scales.

***

You are now almost halfway through your quest (see Figure VI.17). As the painter, you achieved the following results in this voyage:

- You **used your magnifying glass to recognize your canvas patterns, painted your current state self-portrait, and identified potential areas of opportunities.**
- You subsequently **started working on your future state self-portrait.** You unleashed the **power of your purpose**, by crafting your **vision** and defining your **spheres of action.**
- Finally, based on your vision and SoA, **you defined, rated, and prioritized your strategic goals**.

Before moving on to the next stage of your quest, where you will assume the avatar of the maestro or maestra, take some time, still as the painter, to review the details of your *Habits Strategic Canvas* in your workbook.

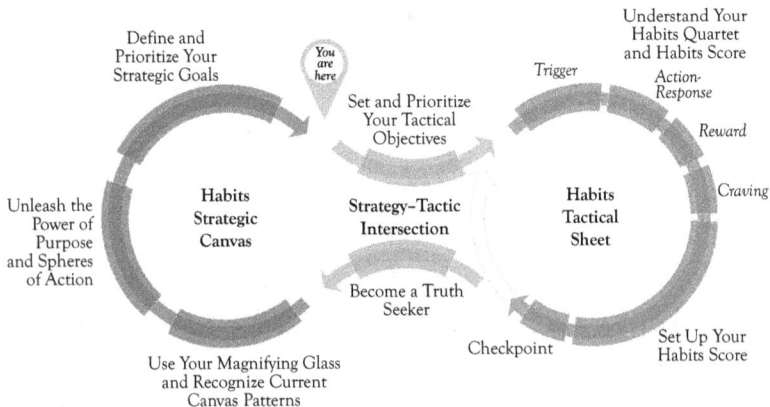

Figure VI.17 Halfway through your quest

PART 4

The Maestro/a

An eminent composer and a conductor, who will coordinate a powerful *Habits Quartet* and compose a repertoire of *Habits Scores* to create the consistency required to build habits.

You've donned the cape of the novice and understood that your quest to create habits implies a multifaceted approach. You learned that you need to assimilate neuroscience insights, incorporate a business management philosophy, leverage your habits growth mindset, and design an environment to facilitate the creation of habits.

As the scientist, you've comprehended the general laws of what makes the brain tick when building or changing habits, why you resist change, and the brain traps and illusions that may trip you as you create habits.

As the painter, you analyzed your beliefs and values. You defined your strong, passionate, and emotional "why"; chose areas of growth; and understood how badly you want to achieve your strategic goals.

You are now at the stage of your quest where you will move from a strategic to a tactical perspective.

For this part of your journey, you will need to assume a maestro or maestra avatar, be this Sir Simon Rattle, Marin Alsop, or any other maestro or maestra of your choice (see Figure 4.1).

In the following voyage, as the maestro or maestra, you will scale down your strategic goals into manageable, bite-size tactical objectives. You will operationalize these objectives by composing and creating a repertoire of *Habits Scores*, a written form of habits compositions, for your *Habits Quartet*.

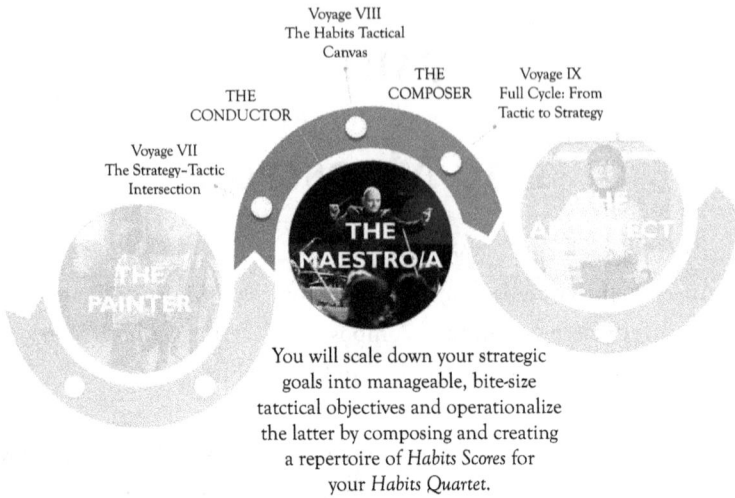

Figure 4.1 Operationalizing your strategy

VOYAGE VII

The Strategy–Tactic Intersection

What you get by achieving your goals is not as important as what you become by achieving your goals.

—Michelangelo Buonarroti, Renaissance artist

On a neural level, the intersection between your strategy (your "big" why) and your tactics (your how) balances the strategic goals of your vision with your habit formation process.

Your **objectives**, in this fundamental intersection, are as follows:

- Understand **how the Habits Formation Matrix overlays your strategy and tactics**.
- **Define your rules of tactical engagement** that orchestrate your strategic goals into tactical objectives. This will impede you from ignoring your tactical objectives or only focusing on your strategy, your desired end state.
- **Define how you will monitor the achievement** of your desired outcome through targets and metrics of success. This is important so that you will not spend all your time executing tactics, losing the connection to your strategy.

***

To achieve these objectives, you will need to execute three missions:

- Mission 23: Set Your Tactical Objectives
- Mission 24: Rate Your Tactical Objectives
- Mission 25: Prioritize Your Objectives

***

To explore this intersecting realm, we give further deliberation to the Habits Formation Matrix and how it overlays the voyages and missions you have executed and will undertake.

Habits Formation Matrix: Strategy and Tactics

You will recall from your mission, *Habits Formation Matrix: An Overview*, that you will experience varying levels of efficiency, automaticity, and flexibility as you transition from new to habitual behavior.

Through the voyages and missions you have undertaken, you will now be able to further understand how this matrix applies to your quest.

You Don't Know You Need to Create a Habit

Stage 1. Unconscious Incompetence

In the first stage of the matrix, you are completely unaware of your incompetence in relation to a specific skill. You are cheerfully ignorant, and your confidence may exceed your capability.

It was with this mindset, when you began your quest, that you undertook several voyages of exploration.

In *Voyage I Creating Habits: Brain Science, Business Thinking, Habits Mindset, and Environmental Contexts*, by accepting the challenge of your quest, you opened yourself to new possibilities.

During the same voyage, you understood that habits are a part of your everyday life. You grasped that to build habits effectively, you need to create a dialogue between neuroscience and psychology, apply business thinking at a personal level, instill a habits growth mindset in yourself, and shape your environment.

As you traveled from the Amazon rainforest to Southern Europe during your second voyage, you realized you have significant potential and options to learn, encode, and process information. It is this connectivity and neuroplasticity that will allow you to build new synaptic connections and strengthen existing synapses.

You also reviewed the four components of habits: the trigger, craving, action-response, and reward.

In *Voyage III Friends or Foes*, you explored the different *Final Frontier* systems. You uncovered insights and brain shortcuts that helped you understand why you resist change and have difficulty in acquiring habits.

During *Voyage IV Identity System—Illusions and Mindset*, you assimilated that not wanting to or being incapable of creating habits may arise from a psychological illusion. You may implicitly assume that your identity is static, and you are perhaps unconsciously creating anchors to maintain the consistency of your *Identity System*.

This state of *unconscious incompetence* may also arise from the difficulty you have in judging how incompetent you are (the Dunning–Kruger effect).

If you were successful at this stage, **you will have recognized your own incompetence by accepting that you may have been blind to potential shortfalls.**

You Know You Need to Create a Habit

Stage 2. Conscious Incompetence

As you continued your journey and reflected upon your *Identity System*, you may have realized the need to acquire certain skills. Because of weakness in certain areas, you recognized the opportunities and the value of creating habits to acquire these skills, which will allow you to achieve higher performance levels.

In this second stage, during your fifth voyage *Strategy and Tactics*, you assumed a painter avatar. You understood the holistic management perspective and approach required to create habits effectively.

In *Voyage VI The Habits Strategic Canvas*, you defined your vision, SoA, and strategic goals that together give you the impetus required to move from stage 2 to stage 3.

It was at this stage that you committed yourself to build new habits, but you may be at odds with your awkwardness, embarrassment, fear, and uncertainty.

To support you in this stage, you will carry out diverse missions in your maestro or maestra avatar, as you scale down your strategic goals into tactical objectives.

In these missions, as you define the objectives associated with the habits you need to create, your brain will process enormous amounts of data through:

- Top–down approximations—driven by your experiences, current context, expectations, interpretations, and biases of your *Identity System*.
- Bottom–up approximations—built from your logically layered objective observations or subjective perceptions of your vision, SoA, and strategic goals.

Brain computational cost will be extremely high during this period, as the new situation is analyzed, and you take decisions on how to respond to external or internal stimuli.

It is at this stage of creating habits that will lead to behavior change—such as improving your leadership skills, team dynamics, or goal setting—that you will require broadened attention and openness to new ideas.

Creating a Habit

Stage 3. Conscious Competence

In the third stage of the matrix, the process of habit formation is experimental, as you practice the new skill.

During this stage, as the maestro or maestra, in the roles of composer and conductor, you will undertake *Voyage VIII The Habits Tactical Sheet*.

You will understand, create, and optimize your *Habits Score* and implement different techniques and tools to get your *Habits Quartet* to play at peak performance.

As you practice skills and acquire knowledge you need, you will feel excited and gain confidence, but there is still **heavy conscious involvement** in executing the new habit.

When encountering this situation, your brain tries to make sense of untested, unestablished ideas, techniques, actions, emotions, or thoughts.

You will need conscious effort and active deliberation, as your action-responses are linked to emotionally relevant outcomes and rewards.

Your Habit Is Now Effortless

Stage 4. Unconscious Competence

With practice, your habit will become second nature, and you will perform it without thinking about it.

Over time, triggers that you define will activate your habitual responses. Your behavior has become automatic, your decision making and choices reflexive, all based on retrospective experiences you created. You **will no longer spend conscious resources** on the habit.

In this stage, as you notice the long-lasting change, your "new habits" will have transitioned to "current habits." Your brain has learned the associations between the components of your *Habits Quartet*.

You will have created new *Habits Scores* neural pathways, and as you hit cruise control, you stop relying on your motivation and willpower.

Now that you've understood the overlay between the Habits Formation Matrix and your quest, in the next mission, you will scale down your strategic goals into tactical objectives.

From Strategic Goals to Tactical Objectives

In your sixth voyage, *The Habits Strategic Canvas*, you unleashed the power of your purpose as you used a systematic process of envisioning your desired future by defining your vision, SoA, and strategic goals.

Your strategic goals are conceptual, are large in scope, and have a long timeframe. They may distract you, as you cannot trust your brain to assess your progress accurately toward these goals.

To circumvent this potential issue, within the strategy–tactic intersection, you need to define the rules of tactical engagement. You do this by orchestrating your strategic goals into tactical objectives or subgoals, to be achieved in a shorter timeframe.

Your tactical objectives are fundamental for diverse reasons. Psychologists and goal-setting specialists Gary Latham and Edwin Locke found across diverse studies that while your strategic goals will help you persist, breaking these into achievable objectives is fundamental to [55]:

- Further sharpen your focus.
- Create certainty, allowing your brain to filter out irrelevant information.
- Increase confidence in achieving your goals.

Embedded within your strategic goals, your tactical objectives effectively create a meaningful bridge between the "how" and the "why" (see Figure VII.1).

Figure VII.1 **A bridge between strategy and tactics**

By breaking your big "why" into "smaller whys" and "how," you will see the finish line of your future *Identity System* at a shorter distance.

This discernment effectively changes your psychological experience. Achieving your "smaller whys" and the associated incremental motivations will prove your capability as you work toward your desired *Identity System*. It will also give you added energy and increase the probability of you focusing on the actions you have set out to do.

Sharpen Your Focus

Imagine, for instance, that part of your ideal future *Identity System* is to leverage your coaching leadership style, to ensure an alignment between your team's goals and the company vision. This is a broad goal. How do you get there?

You will need to break this strategic goal down into smaller tactical objectives. How can you demonstrate this leadership style? You can, for example, set up a mentoring program you will monitor through the number of times you hold effective weekly mentoring sessions with your team members.

In Figure VII.2, for the example mentioned earlier, you can compare the components of your tactical objectives with your strategic goals.

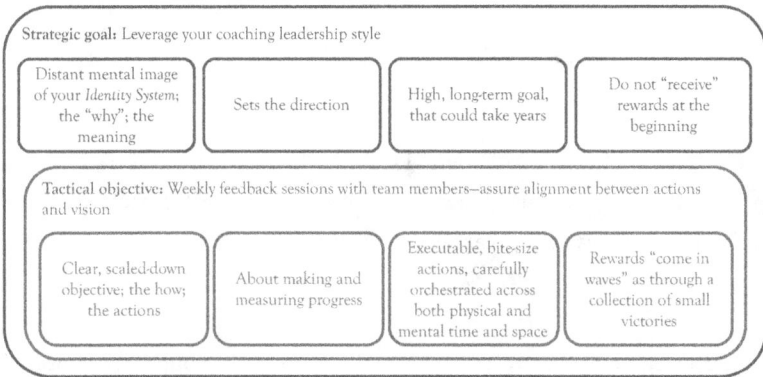

Strategic goal: Leverage your coaching leadership style

| Distant mental image of your *Identity System*; the "why"; the meaning | Sets the direction | High, long-term goal, that could take years | Do not "receive" rewards at the beginning |

Tactical objective: Weekly feedback sessions with team members–assure alignment between actions and vision

| Clear, scaled-down objective; the how; the actions | About making and measuring progress | Executable, bite-size actions, carefully orchestrated across both physical and mental time and space | Rewards "come in waves" as through a collection of small victories |

Figure VII.2 From strategic goals to tactical objectives

Michael's Strategic Goals and Tactical Objectives

To further understand this breakdown, compare Michael's goals and objectives in Table VII.1.

Table VII.1 Michael's strategic goals and tactical objectives

Strategic Goal	Tactical Objective
Within six months, I will fully understand my emotions and their impact on relationships	I will practice and cultivate essential skills daily to regulate my emotions
Within six months, I will manage my emotions constructively to leverage performance	I will positively power all disturbing impulses in potential threat situations and keep them in check as these arise

***

🚀 Mission 23: Set Your Tactical Objectives

Based on the components and examples described earlier, you can now define your tactical objectives. Use the template provided in the workbook to complete this mission. Once defined, you will be ready to assess and prioritize your objectives.

***

Assess Your Tactical Objectives

Now that you have defined your tactical objectives, you will evaluate these against various fundamental criteria. Use your workbook to complete the rating of your objectives. The logic of this exercise will be familiar to you, as you've carried out a similar mission for your strategic goals:

1. The first criterion to consider is the number of your tactical objectives. You will then review each objective selected against the following criteria:
2. Alignment with your strategic goals.
3. Simple, clear, and easy to recall.
4. Emotionally relevant.
5. Effort you will put in.
6. Approach versus avoidance-oriented tactical objectives.
7. Challenging tactical objectives with short timescales.
8. Results oriented and meaningfully measurable tactical objectives.

***

🚀 Mission 24: Rate Your Tactical Objectives

You should now review each criterion for your tactical objectives. As you review each criterion, Michael will also share his output with you where relevant.

1. **Is the number of my tactical objectives limited?**

   While many possible tactical objectives answer the "how" question, you need to remember the constraints of your executive system's cognitive capacity. You should have a maximum of two to three objectives for each of your strategic goals. Rate the first criterion using the scale shown in Figure VII.3.

Are my tactical objectives limited in number?									
1	2	3	4	5	6	7	8	9	10

1 = Too many objectives; 5 = Can reduce number; 10 = Just correct.

Figure VII.3 Number of tactical objectives

In Michael's case, he has opted to have one objective for each strategic goal.

Now, for each of your tactical objectives, review the following criteria.

2. **Is my tactical objective important? Does it provide meaning to my strategic goal?**

   Your tactical objectives need to be meaningful and contribute to achieving your strategic goals. Rate this objective using the scale shown in Figure VII.4.

Is my tactical objective important to me? Does it provide meaning to my strategic goal?									
1	2	3	4	5	6	7	8	9	10

1 = Low importance; 5 = Moderate importance; 10 = High importance.

Figure VII.4 Importance of tactical objectives

In Michael's case, there is a clear alignment between his objectives and his strategic goals, as shown in Table VII.1.

3. **Is my tactical objective simple, clear, and easy to recall?**

Clear objectives are important because they tell you where and when to focus your attention. Your mind doesn't have to wonder about what to do next—it already knows.

Remember, your objectives will need to stick like glue in your memory. Rate this criterion using the scale shown in Figure VII.5.

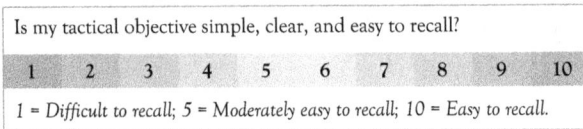

Is my tactical objective simple, clear, and easy to recall?									
1	2	3	4	5	6	7	8	9	10

1 = Difficult to recall; 5 = Moderately easy to recall; 10 = Easy to recall.

Figure VII.5 Glue-like tactical objectives

In Michael's case, the words "... cultivate essential skills ..." and "... positively power all disturbing impulses ..." are simple and stick like glue.

4. **Do emotions drive my tactical objective?**

Is emotional fuel driving your tactical objectives? Are you excited? Does the challenge motivate you? If you don't feel strongly about the objective, you will need to change it entirely. Rate each objective using the scale shown in Figure VII.6.

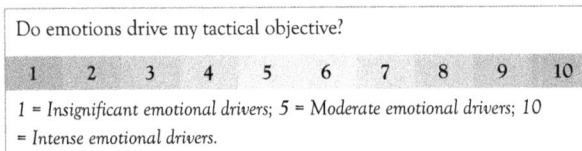

Do emotions drive my tactical objective?									
1	2	3	4	5	6	7	8	9	10

1 = Insignificant emotional drivers; 5 = Moderate emotional drivers; 10 = Intense emotional drivers.

Figure VII.6 Emotional relevance of tactical objectives

The glue-like characteristics of Michael's tactical objective phrases "... cultivate essential skills ..." and "... positively power all disturbing impulses ..." clearly drive the emotional tone in his goals.

5. **How much effort will I put in to achieve my tactical objective?**

How important is the objective? Are you determined? How much effort will you put in? Rate this criterion on the scale shown in Figure VII.7.

How much effort will I put in to achieve my tactical objective?									
1	2	3	4	5	6	7	8	9	10

1 = Will not expend any effort; 5 = Will put in some effort;
10 = Will give it all I've got.

Figure VII.7 Tactical objective and effort level

6. **Is my tactical objective approach oriented?**

Are your objectives framed to your *Identity System* traits? Recall that your mindset can either be approach or avoidance based. Rate this criterion using the scale shown in Figure VII.8.

Is my tactical objective framed to my *Identity System* traits?									
1	2	3	4	5	6	7	8	9	10

1 = Objectives not framed to Identity System traits;
10 = Objectives framed to Identity System traits

Figure VII.8 Tactical objectives and mindset traits

If your objectives are avoidance mindset oriented, consider setting these using an approach mindset. Rate this criterion using the scale shown in Figure VII.9.

Do I have an avoidance or approach mindset?									
1	2	3	4	5	6	7	8	9	10

1 = Avoidance mindset; 10 = Approach mindset.

Figure VII.9 Tactical objectives and mindset

7. **Is my tactical objective challenging and does it have a short timescale?**

Think of challenging, yet manageable objectives. Rate this criterion using the scale shown in Figure VII.10.

Is my tactical objective challenging?									
1	2	3	4	5	6	7	8	9	10

1 = Nonstretch objectives; 5 = Can incorporate more stretch;
10 = Stretch just right.

Figure VII.10 Challenging tactical objectives

Your attention will need to be on the clear objective you have set and not the high goal. Shorter timescales will help you get this right. Rate this criterion using the scale shown in Figure VII.11.

Does my tactical objective have a short timescale?									
1	2	3	4	5	6	7	8	9	10

1 = Actions cannot be executed in a short timeframe;
10 = Actions can be executed in a short timeframe.

Figure VII.11 Tactical objectives with a short timescale

> Both of Michael's tactical objectives are challenging and have short timescales ("… on a daily basis …" and "… as these arise …").

8. **Is my tactical objective results oriented and meaningfully measurable?**

Are you measuring your actions or milestones rather than the outcome? As stated by Stacey Barr, one of the foremost performance measurement, KPI (Key Performance Indicator), and evidence-based leadership experts, you need to ensure that you separate your goals from your actions and your measure from your targets (each of these elements is important to single out).

> Both of Michael's tactical objectives are results oriented:
>
> "… to regulate my emotions …"
> "… positively power all disturbing impulses … keep them in check …"

You should write your goals so that they are results oriented. Rate this criterion using the scale shown in Figure VII.12.

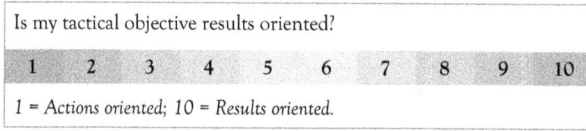

Is my tactical objective results oriented?									
1	2	3	4	5	6	7	8	9	10

1 = Actions oriented; 10 = Results oriented.

Figure VII.12 Results-oriented objectives

Focusing on the measurability of your tactical objectives is also fundamental. This will merge your awareness and action, tighten your concentration, and heighten your motivation, and you will be able to filter out extraneous information.

At this stage, all that is required is your appreciation of the measurability of your objectives, as you will tackle this point in some depth in *Voyage IX Full Cycle—From Tactics to Strategy*, where you will define specific measures and targets.

Rate this criterion using the scale shown in Figure VII.13.

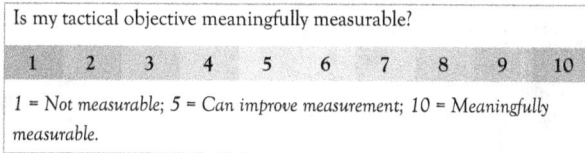

Is my tactical objective meaningfully measurable?									
1	2	3	4	5	6	7	8	9	10

1 = Not measurable; 5 = Can improve measurement; 10 = Meaningfully measurable.

Figure VII.13 Meaningfully measurable objectives

> Michael's appreciation of his tactical objectives is that they are both meaningfully measurable. He is sure that he can set both measures and targets for both of his objectives.

***

🚀 Mission 25: Prioritize Your Objectives

Now that you have assessed the different criteria in relation to your objectives, the next step is to prioritize your objectives. This will reduce your uncertainty, psychological costs, and cognitive load.

Review the average criteria score for each tactical objective in your workbook.

If you have objectives with competing total scores, define a second level of prioritization, for example, prioritizing the goals where you ranked highest on the effort and emotional scales.

***

In your first voyage as the maestro or maestra, you achieved the following results:

- You **understood how the Habits Formation Matrix overlays your strategy and tactics**.
- You have **defined, rated, and prioritized your tactical objectives**.

You are now ready to set up your *Habits Scores* for your *Habits Quartet* (see Figure VII.14, point A).

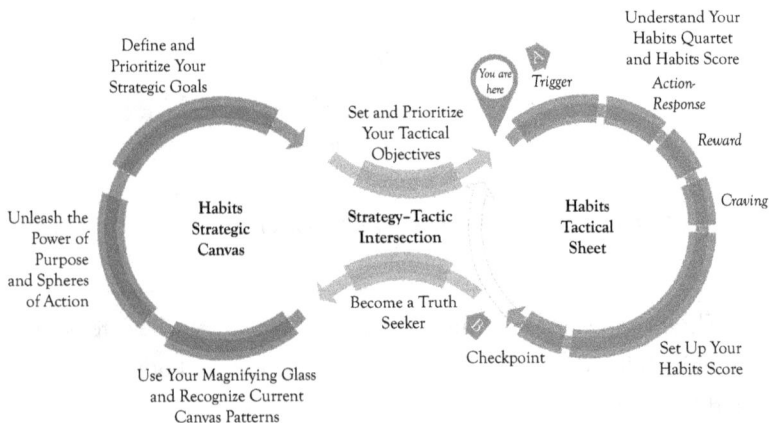

Figure VII.14 Operationalizing your tactics

At this stage, you may feel that you would like to obtain a general understanding of the logic of setting up measures and targets for your strategic goals and tactical objectives.

If so, before continuing your journey, you can warp speed to *Voyage IX Full Cycle—From Tactics to Strategy* and review the section *Monitor Your Strategy and Habits* (see Figure VII.14, point B), before initiating *Voyage VIII The Habits Tactical Sheet* (point A).

VOYAGE VIII

The Habits Tactical Sheet

Creating habits is much like conducting a great orchestra, in which each player listens to the other instruments as they play their score.

In the prior voyage, as the maestro or maestra, you orchestrated your vision and strategic goals into manageable and prioritized tactical objectives.

In this voyage, in the same role, to operationalize your tactics, your **objectives** are:

- ⊕ **Understand the components of the *Habits Quartet*** that will need to work together for successful habit creation.
- ⊕ **Create *Habits Scores* for your *Habits Quartet***, to ensure the alignment and consistency required to build habits.

***

To achieve these objectives, you will need to execute 16 missions:

- 🚀 Mission 26: Understand the Emotional Trigger
- 🚀 Mission 27: Identify Current Event Triggers
- 🚀 Mission 28: Identify Current Time-Based Triggers
- 🚀 Mission 29: Identify Current Location/Object Triggers
- 🚀 Mission 30: Understand People Triggers
- 🚀 Mission 31: Create an Arsenal of Triggers
- 🚀 Mission 32: Understand Your Action-Responses
- 🚀 Mission 33: Identify Current Rewards
- 🚀 Mission 34: Understand Your Current Cravings
- 🚀 Mission 35: Define Your Action-Responses
- 🚀 Mission 36: Create a Habits Pyramid
- 🚀 Mission 37: Define Your Triggers

🚀 Mission 38: Create Your Instant Habits
🚀 Mission 39: Define Your Rewards
🚀 Mission 40: Define Your Cravings
🚀 Mission 41: Habits Score Checkpoint

***

Your *Habits Quartet*—Current Habits

When you began your first voyage *From the Amazon Rainforest to Europe*, you read about the four components of the *Habits Quartet*. Recall the to-do list example, shown in Table VIII.1.

Table VIII.1 To-do list example

Quartet	Example
Trigger	To-do list
Craving	Anticipation that is felt. The brain releases dopamine in expectation of a reward
Action-response	Review/update the to-do list first thing in the morning and during the day
Reward	Feeling satisfied by being better prepared for your workday. Release of the chemical dopamine, which plays a fundamental role in motivating behavior

For your current habits, your *Habits Quartet* (see Figure VIII.1) **has come under the control of your automatic and nonconscious mind**—you are unconsciously competent as you perform these habits.

When this happens, your neurotransmitters (your chemical messengers) fire as follows (see Figure VIII.2):

1. Your brain (unconsciously) identifies a trigger.
2. Your neurons will fire chemical messengers (e.g., dopamine) as your cravings intensify.
3. As you execute your action-response, the neurons firing diminishes.
4. When you experience the reward, your neurons will fire again.

For your current habits, the peaks of neurons firing and releasing neurotransmitters, in a brain region involved in habit formation, occur

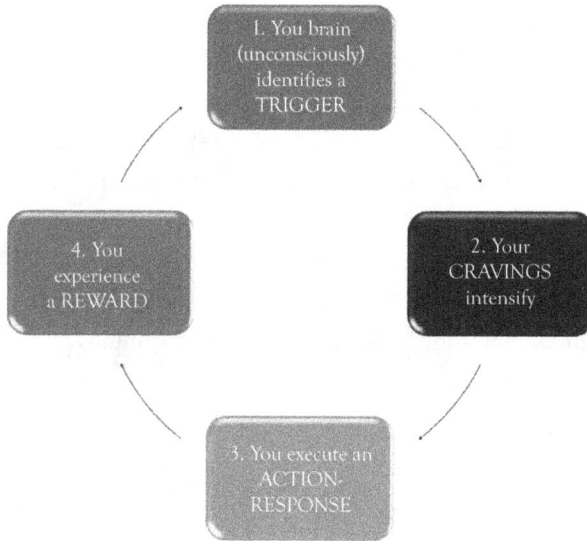

Figure VIII.1 The Habits Quartet

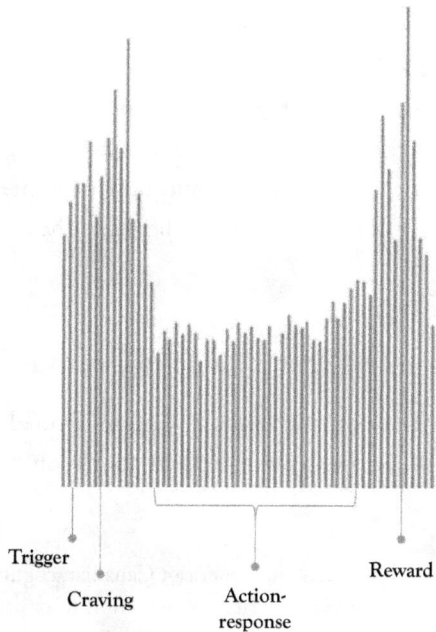

Figure VIII.2 Firing of neurons for current habits

at the beginning and the end of habitual behavior [56], while the trough occurs throughout the action-response.

Let's look at another example.

You are under pressure to resolve diverse problems at work. You are overburdened and feel that you need to solve all the problems quickly.

1. Trigger: Your e-mail pings with a new message.
2. Craving: You immediately feel the urge to check your e-mail, as your brain is constantly looking for an external stimulus.
3. Action-response: You check your e-mail and read recent messages to see if you've missed any information you might need.
4. Reward: You satisfy your craving to multitask[1]. Multitasking becomes connected with feeling overburdened, anxious, and resolving problems.

Throughout this four-step process, learning has happened all along the way as through experience, your brain identifies outcomes following your response, registers relevant triggers and cravings, and encodes and catalogs habits for future use in your Habits System. The creation and execution of your habits is the intrinsic result of this brain–body neurobiological feedback loop in action.

To further understand this perspective of habit creation, you will carry out various missions, where you will explore each component of your *Habits Quartet*. You will understand how they interact with each other, and why creating an alignment between these components is fundamental.

Trigger—The Instantaneous Opening Move

Triggers, real or perceived, are prompts or cues captured by your senses that "urge" your brain to respond to a specific situation.

---

[1] As referred to by Daniel J. Levitin, American Canadian cognitive psychologist and neuroscientist, "Multitasking creates an addiction to dopamine, through a feedback loop that rewards the brain for losing focus and constantly looking for an external stimulus."

As the maestro or maestra, you can think of triggers as the instantaneous opening moves that prompt your action-responses.

The generic categories for triggers are shown in Table VIII.2.

Table VIII.2 Trigger categories

Category
A preceding or subsequent event
Time-based
Location/object
People
Emotion

In the to-do list and e-mail examples, the to-do list trigger falls within the object category and the e-mail in the preceding event category.

In the following sections, we will look at each category, starting with the emotions category. Understanding this trigger category will allow you to fully grasp the intricate "subconscious characteristics" of triggers.

Emotion

Most of the time, you are not aware of your emotional, subconscious triggers. Just like Michael, we can all relate to the experience of thinking along the lines, "I can't believe I just reacted that way" or "I can't believe I just said that."

In these situations, your risk analysis system (see *Voyage III: Friends or Foes*) has overridden your executive system.

Having instantaneously identified a potential threat from input by the senses, an alarm bell has gone off in your risk analysis system. It reacts to the perceived threat instantaneously, diverting energy from your executive system and triggering your emotional response.

In these situations, your brain can go into autopilot emotional action-response mode.

The trigger—being addressed by a colleague in a rude tone—leads to an instantaneous fight-or-flight action-response. The associated "to be safe or to dominate" reward has become so entwined that a powerful sensation of apprehension emerges as adrenaline is injected into the bloodstream.

From a brain–body feedback loop perspective, in your emotional response to a threat situation, what happens?

Your risk analysis system takes just one quarter of a second to identify the trigger and another one quarter of a second to send signals from your brain to your adrenal glands [57]. These glands, sitting on top of your kidneys, produce and discharge adrenaline into your bloodstream instantaneously.

Your action-response takes place just half a second after the trigger!

With this **high level of response automaticity, the conscious gap between the trigger and the action-response is practically nonexistent, and your action-responses occur in autopilot mode** (see Figure VIII.3).

Trigger ▶▶ | ▶▶ Action-response

The conscious gap between the trigger and the action-response is practically nonexistent	Occurs almost spontaneously. On autopilot, your action-response is "chosen" by your subconsciousness

Figure VIII.3 Emotion trigger and action-response

Paraphrasing Viktor Frankl,[2] "there is a gap between the trigger and emotional action-response, and in that gap, exists your power to define and choose your habit."

Now that you are aware of how emotional triggers function, you are ready to execute your next mission.

***

🚀 Mission 26: Understand the Emotional Trigger

In this mission, recall emotional events (e.g., being addressed by a colleague in a rude tone; your boss requesting a meeting at 5 p.m. on a

---

[2] Austrian neurologist, psychiatrist, philosopher, writer, and Holocaust survivor.

THE HABITS TACTICAL SHEET   119

Friday; being praised or criticized in front of your colleagues) and answer the following questions, documenting these in your workbook.

- What situations activated your response?
- Was it being disagreed with, dismissed, or diminished or was it pride in the face of recognition?
- When emotionally triggered, how quickly did you respond, and what was your first response or combination of responses?
- Did you respond with away states of fighting, fleeing, freezing, flocking, or appeasing, or were your actions related to toward states of acceptance, feeling energized and engaged?
- Were you able to recognize your sentiments after these events, and how did these affect you?

***

This exercise is an important first step to understanding response automaticity (see Figure VIII.4). Seeing your patterns of automatic emotional action-responses, understanding the triggers that activated these, and the resulting impact of away or toward states is a great way to start creating and changing habits based on emotional triggers.

You should learn to listen to, rather than suppress or react to, emotion triggers. These are important signals from your subconscious, data that you need to diagnose, to choose your action-response.

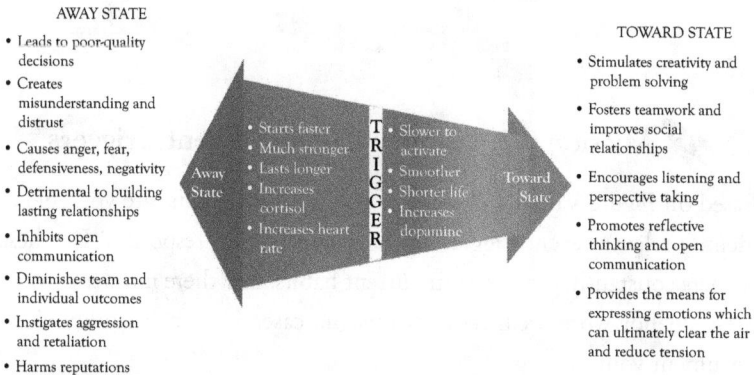

AWAY STATE
- Leads to poor-quality decisions
- Creates misunderstanding and distrust
- Causes anger, fear, defensiveness, negativity
- Detrimental to building lasting relationships
- Inhibits open communication
- Diminishes team and individual outcomes
- Instigates aggression and retaliation
- Harms reputations

TOWARD STATE
- Stimulates creativity and problem solving
- Fosters teamwork and improves social relationships
- Encourages listening and perspective taking
- Promotes reflective thinking and open communication
- Provides the means for expressing emotions which can ultimately clear the air and reduce tension

Away State

TRIGGER
- Starts faster
- Much stronger
- Lasts longer
- Increases cortisol
- Increases heart rate
- Slower to activate
- Smoother
- Shorter life
- Increases dopamine

Toward State

Figure VIII.4 Emotional triggers and states

Event

Many of your habits are an automatic response to hundreds of event-based triggers that occur throughout your day.

Examples of potential event-based triggers, from the moment you wake up to the moment you get back into bed at night, are shown in Figure VIII.5.

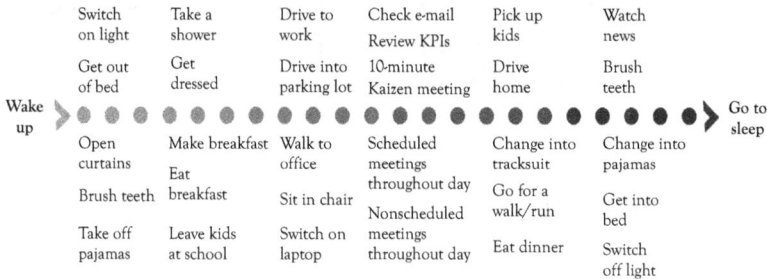

	Switch on light	Take a shower	Drive to work	Check e-mail / Review KPIs	Pick up kids	Watch news	
	Get out of bed	Get dressed	Drive into parking lot	10-minute Kaizen meeting	Drive home	Brush teeth	
Wake up	● ●						**Go to sleep**
	Open curtains	Make breakfast / Eat breakfast	Walk to office	Scheduled meetings throughout day	Change into tracksuit / Go for a walk/run	Change into pajamas / Get into bed	
	Brush teeth	Leave kids at school	Sit in chair / Switch on laptop	Nonscheduled meetings throughout day	Eat dinner	Switch off light	
	Take off pajamas						

Figure VIII.5 Event-based triggers

The **potential events that can precede or follow your action-responses and that you can use as triggers are endless. It is important to understand and experiment with these,** to learn which is more suitable for the habit you want to build.

An example of a preceding event-based trigger is:

Event trigger → Action-response
Switch on your laptop → Review KPI dashboard

***

🚀 Mission 27: Identify Current Event Triggers

Based on Figure VIII.5 and some of your current habits, are you able to identify relevant event triggers and associated action-responses? Do these triggers constantly prompt your current habits? Are there moments when these do not work well? Why is this the case? Use your workbook to document your findings.

***

Time-Based

Time-based triggers are powerful and work well for people with 9 to 5 jobs and structured schedules, as they carry out specific activities at similar times each day or on specific days during the week.

Time-based triggers are useful for creating habits, as they have a recurring pattern. They give your brain the certainty it requires in helping you implement your action-response and build discipline.

You can use digital reminders, calendar events, alarms, or app notifications for time-based triggers, be these specific times during the day or specific days during the week.

These triggers need to be used with ponderation, as they are rigid with low flexibility and little ambiguity. If your schedule is flexible, this category may not be the correct one to use.

Examples of time-based triggers are:

Time trigger → Action-response

Habit app time trigger → Notification sent to execute an action-response at a specific time

Recurring calendar event → A reminder 15 minutes before the action-response

Note: A useful functionality of these time-based apps is the "snooze mode" that you can select until you execute the action-response.

***

🚀 Mission 28: Identify Current Time-Based Triggers

Are you able to identify relevant time-based triggers for your current habits? Do these triggers prompt your current habits? Are there moments when these do not work well? Why is this the case? Use your workbook to document your findings.

***

Location/Object

Most of the time, your habits and behaviors are a product of your habitual locations or those that, though you do not frequent regularly, elicit habitual responses given their similarity.

As you normally carry out your habits in familiar environments, a useful technique is to adapt your environments (or objects in your environments) to facilitate creating habits. We will delve into this point in *Voyage X: Taking Habits to the Next Level.*

Objects are physical items within the locations you frequent that trigger your action-response.

Examples of location/object-based triggers are:

Location/object-based triggers → Action-response
    Office/chair/to-do list next to laptop → Review and complete to-do list

As you can see, physical reminders and locations where you execute your routines make it effortless to start building habits.

***

🚀 Mission 29: Identify Current Location/ Object Triggers

Are you able to identify relevant locations or objects that trigger your current habits? In which locations do your habits occur? Which objects spur your actions? What are the characteristics of these that lead you to carry out the habit? Do these triggers constantly prompt your current habits? Are there moments when these do not work well? Why is this the case? Use your workbook to document your findings.

***

Other People

Over time, within your business and social environments, your peers, colleagues, and friends may become the primary predictors of your habits and behaviors. This can lead to both positive and negative behaviors and attitudes. We will review this point further in *Voyage X: Taking Habits to the Next Level.*

***

🚀 Mission 30: Understand People Triggers

Are you able to identify relevant groups or people that trigger or encourage your current habits? Are these positive or negative habits? What people characteristics lead you to carry out the habit? Do these triggers constantly prompt your current habits? Are there moments when these do not work well? Why is this the case? Use your workbook to document your findings.

***

Trigger Criteria

To change or create habits, as you've just seen, you first need to notice and identify the (potential) triggers that (will) activate your action-responses.

This ability to define relevant triggers is the foundation for every action-response you will need to execute.

Once you've identified your triggers, determine their effectiveness using the ACIDS test. Your triggers should be:

- **A**ctionable—you can act upon them.
- **C**onsistent—should happen with reliable frequency.
- **I**nescapable—unavoidable.
- **D**istinct—clearly defined or identifiable.
- **S**pontaneous—occur automatically, on their own, without effort.

***

🚀 Mission 31: Create an Arsenal of Triggers

In the business world, where the only certainty is constant change and demanding schedules, for your *Habits Quartet* to perform well, you will need to create an arsenal of triggers.

This arsenal will need to include multiple, flexible, and/or structured triggers. You will need to adjust your exposure to these, to activate your action-response as required.

With repeated reinforcement, the association between the triggers in your arsenal and the action-responses will strengthen.

1. Think of a habit you currently have or one you would like to create.
2. Can you identify the trigger that activates the action-response?
3. Based on the ACIDS test, can you improve this trigger or use other triggers? Are your triggers:
   • Actionable—can you act upon it?
   • Consistent—does it happen with reliable frequency? Can you increase the frequency or consistency of the trigger?
   • Inescapable—is the trigger unavoidable?
   • Distinct—is it identifiable?
   • Spontaneous—does it occur automatically?
4. Do you need to increase or eliminate your exposure to your triggers?
5. Can you create multiple triggers for the action-response?
6. Have you considered all the categories? Which are the most applicable?

***

Action-Response—Focused Tempo

The action-response is the behavior you perform after the trigger. This can be a mental, emotional, or physical action-response.

Whether an action-response occurs and repeats over time depends on diverse factors. These include how well the *Habits Quartet* components play together and your capability to fully focus your attention on the action-responses.

From Action-Response Potential to Focused Performance

In relation to the latter aspect, you will recollect from your travels through the Amazon rainforest and over southern Europe how neurons function and the fundamental contribution of this building block to habit formation.

You also learned about Hebb's law, which states that when neurons are activated repeatedly within the same pattern, a brain circuit will form in time.

Imagine two neurons communicating, let's call them neuron 1 and neuron 2 (see Figure VIII.6).

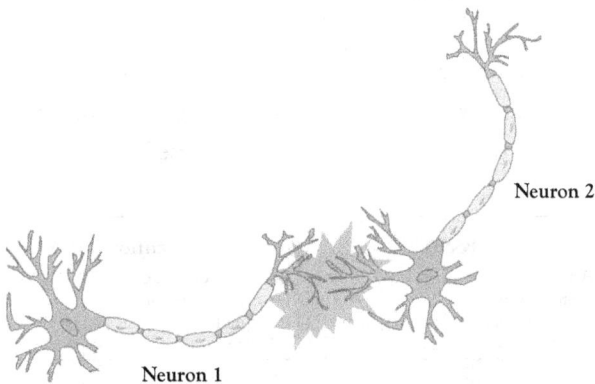

Figure VIII.6 Action potential

For neuron 2 to be activated to receive a message, it needs to receive many signals from neuron 1 and other neurons, until it exceeds a particular threshold.

When this happens, neuron 2 sends its electrical impulse—*an action potential*—along its axon (trunk) to the next neuron in the chain.

Neuron 2 will recharge and fire more frequently if the strength of the stimulus from neuron 1 and other cells is strong and will fire less often if the stimulus is weak.

How can you ensure sufficient intensity to activate neurons repeatedly in the same pattern to form a brain pathway?

For the action-potential to be transformed into stabilized brain circuits, **you will need to focus your attention on the execution of the action-response.**

For the effect of clarity, the following definitions will prevail (see Figure VIII.7):

- Focus: Act of directing your center of interest to relevant stimuli or action responses
- Attention: The depth or level of intensity directed at the stimuli or action-responses
- Focused attention density: Your ability to focus your attention on target stimuli for an extended period

To create new neural pathways, you need to focus all your attention deliberately as you execute your action-response. Your focused attention density needs to be fully directed and not dispersed.

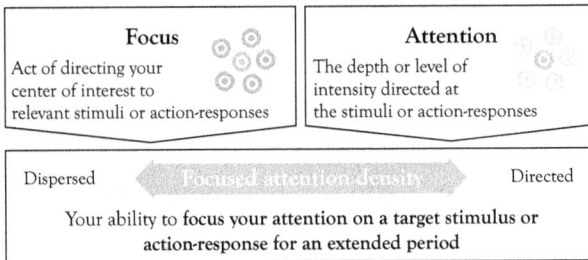

Focus	Attention
Act of directing your center of interest to relevant stimuli or action-responses	The depth or level of intensity directed at the stimuli or action-responses

Dispersed	Focused attention density	Directed

Your ability to focus your attention on a target stimulus or action-response for an extended period

Figure VIII.7 Focused attention density

To support you in this activity, Michael's action-responses represent some solutions you can implement to augment your focused attention density (see *Mission 35: Define Your Action-Responses*).

With practice, over time, you will recognize when ruminating thoughts are attempting to take over, and you can veto or suppress them.

***

🚀 Mission 32: Understand Your Action-Responses

Reflect upon the following questions:

- For the specific action-response of some of your current habits, do you execute the action-response without giving it much thought?

- What conscious effort was involved when you practiced new ways of thinking or working, in creating habits?
- Was your focused attention density directed or dispersed?
- Were you able to capture ruminating thoughts during your action-response?

***

Rewards—The Encore

In your earlier voyages and missions, you decided to create or change a habit to reap the benefits of building a better, stronger, more disciplined version of your *Identity System.*

These **long-term benefits may motivate you** to create or change a habit, but the delayed temporal proximity between your action-response and the benefits **will not sustain the momentum** of repeating the action-response (see Figure VIII.8).

Your **long-term motivation is not effective in your day-to-day**, as your habits are mainly internalized through the desired and immediate positive outcomes and experiences of your action-responses—your short-term rewards [58].

Evidence suggests that the human brain processes immediate rewards and delayed benefits differently [59]. The delayed temporal proximity of the long-term benefit may also lead to temporal discounting, the phenomenon in which the subjective value of the reward loses its magnitude when delayed.

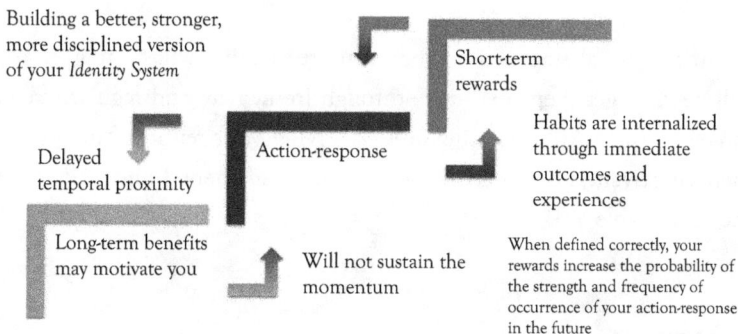

Building a better, stronger, more disciplined version of your *Identity System*

Short-term rewards

Delayed temporal proximity

Action-response

Habits are internalized through immediate outcomes and experiences

Long-term benefits may motivate you

Will not sustain the momentum

When defined correctly, your rewards increase the probability of the strength and frequency of occurrence of your action-response in the future

Figure VIII.8 From long-term benefits to short-term rewards

When defined correctly, your rewards increase the probability of the strength and frequency of occurrence of your action-response in the future [60].

How can you potentiate your reward system?

When you identify and define rewards, you will need to consider which reward, or reward category, may be applicable for your action-response. You can use the classification and examples shown in the list as a starting point.

- **Social rewards**. These can include positive verbal and nonverbal rewards, including feelings, behaviors, and gestures, that will activate your predisposition toward the psychological ownership of your action-response [61].

  This reward is about voicing your support for yourself and others and can include simple gestures such as a smile, a thumbs-up, or a hug. Offering meaningful praise to a colleague or yourself for completing a complex task, expressing sincere empathy, and showing your faith in others ("this is my high-performing team") or yourself are powerful social rewards.
- **Psychological rewards**. These can be something as simple as crossing off a task from the to-do list. Just like social rewards, these will affect your mental and emotional states.
- **Physical rewards.** More tangible, these rewards can include team-building exercises to foster team spirit or going for a brisk walk to energize yourself, after an intense meeting.

In the initial stages, the habits you are creating will be fragile. You will need to get them to "stick" through immediate and regularly reinforced rewards. After defining and classifying your rewards, understand their effectiveness by considering different fundamental dimensions,[3] as shown in Table VIII.3.

---

[3] A key article "A Multidimensional View on Social and Non-Social Rewards" deserves special recognition for their influence in this section [62].

Table VIII.3 Reward dimensions

Temporal proximity	Duration	Emotional intensity
An ultrafast neurobiological feedback loop will help your brain process good feelings to form a habit. Your reward should happen during or milliseconds after the behavior	The transitory nature of the reward needs to be considered. Praising a colleague in private will last a short time. The same act in a public setting will have a longer-lasting effect	This factor is key for action-response repetition. Celebrating the completion of your action-response, for example, triggers positive emotions such as excitement and triumph
Novelty	**Intrinsic/extrinsic**	**Tangibility**
Novelty is a powerful signal for your brain, to determine what you pay attention to. Note that it may have an opposite effect in the social environment, where familiar and relevant faces are more rewarding than faces of strangers [62]	Consider whether the nature of the reward is intrinsic (i.e., originates internally within a person, e.g., feeling satisfied) or is extrinsic (originates externally, e.g., receiving praise) In your case, which of these results in a repetition of the action-response for specific situations?	Rewards can be tangible (concrete, visible, and measurable) or intangible, more abstract (psychological, nonmaterialistic) Which of these works better for you?

***

🚀 Mission 33: Identify Current Rewards

This is an important mission. Take your time to identify and classify specific rewards for some of your current action-responses in your workbook.

1. Describe your reward _____

   For example, from a toward state perspective, "I will get ... progress, incentives, compensation, mastery, reputation, growth, recognition ..." or from an away state perspective, "I will avoid ...punishment, failure ..."

2. Understand the category of your reward:

Social	Psychological	Physical	Other (specify)

3. Describe the dimension:

Temporal proximity (immediate/delayed)	
Duration (short lived/medium/long)	
Emotional intensity (low/medium/high)	
Novelty (novel/familiar)	
Nature (intrinsic/extrinsic)	
Tangibility (tangible/intangible)	

Setting up and understanding your rewards will allow you to adjust these or include other, more powerful rewards.

***

You will now need to comprehend the cravings associated with the rewards you will obtain from executing the action-response.

Cravings—The Rise to Crescendo: Preliminary Encore

You've seen in your voyage through your brain systems that your risk analysis system is continuously monitoring which actions create toward or away states.

As your brain systems associate triggers and action-responses with specific, immediate, and reinforced rewards, your cravings will begin to form. This is part of the neurobiological mechanism that closes the feedback loop to help your brain solidify the neural pathways of your habits.

Cravings result from millions of years of programming of biological and neurological mechanisms[4] into the brain.

Your cravings will rise in crescendo as the trigger activates your brain. Neurotransmitters fire and lock together, and you can almost imagine yourself experiencing the reward. Cravings are hard to resist as your risk analysis, habits, and reward systems will work in unison to bypass your executive system.

To strengthen the link between the benefits of your future *Identity System* and your daily habits, **you need to guarantee that the rewards you define reinforce the association between the trigger and action-response** through the activation of your cravings.

As you've seen in your earlier voyages, your neurotransmitters have a major impact on all aspects of your life and play a fundamental role in regulating many of your neurobiological processes, including cognitive, social, and emotional processes, such as motivation, learning, memory, punishment, and aversion, and your ability to focus, concentrate, and handle anger and stress.

---

[4] You will recall from your voyages as a scientist that cravings are essentially neurotransmitters or chemical messengers.

Your cravings are a manifest of deeper underlying motives. They can be positive, moving you toward rewards, as you anticipate the feelings of pleasure, joy, excitement, or satisfaction. Or they can be negative, moving you away from threats, as you become apprehensive, angry, frustrated, or anxious (see Figure VIII.9).

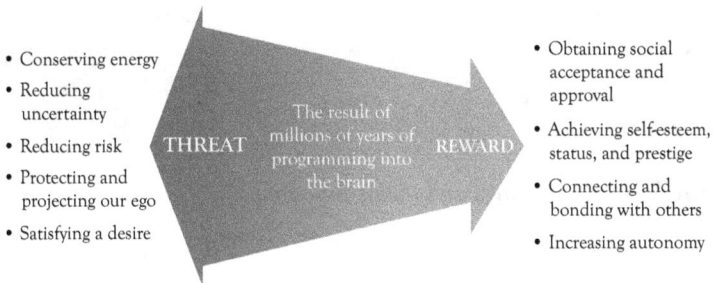

- Conserving energy
- Reducing uncertainty
- Reducing risk
- Protecting and projecting our ego
- Satisfying a desire

THREAT   The result of millions of years of programming into the brain   REWARD

- Obtaining social acceptance and approval
- Achieving self-esteem, status, and prestige
- Connecting and bonding with others
- Increasing autonomy

Figure VIII.9 Cravings—from threats to rewards

A crucial point to note is that the way individuals process threats or rewards will differ.

Each person's thoughts, feelings, and emotions will transform a trigger into potentially different cravings or intensities of cravings. Your boss's attitude may anger you, but your colleague, based on the same trigger, may only feel slightly irritated.

To get your *Habits Quartet* to perform, you need to have a general understanding of the cravings—the potential different neurotransmitters and hormones at play—that the reward will lead to.

Take dopamine, for example. Much has been written about this chemical as a major influencer of your habits, as it plays a fundamental role in pleasure, motivation, and learning.

But dopamine is just one chemical that influences your habits and behaviors. Every behavior involves multiple brain systems, neurotransmitters and other chemicals and hormones, as shown[5] in a sample of neurotransmitters in Figure VIII.10.

Scientists have discovered over 100 of these chemical messengers and they will certainly find more [14].

---

[5] Figure VIII.10 provides a simplistic view of the functions of neurotransmitters. For example, dopamine, apart from motivation and pleasure, plays a role in maintaining memory, attention, learning, and even regulating body movements.

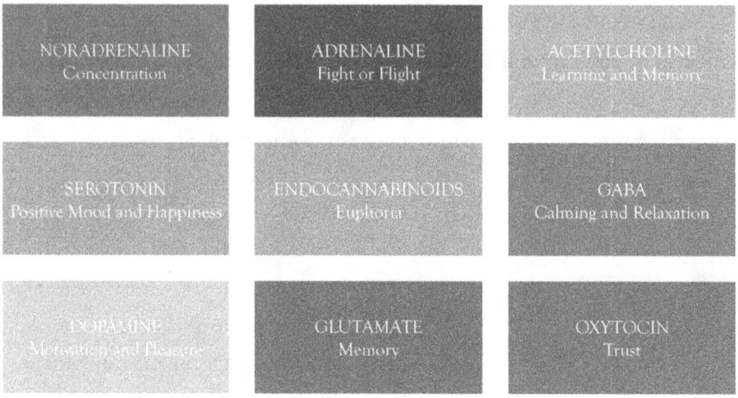

Figure VIII.10 Cravings and major functions

Habits are powerful because of these neurobiological cravings. They can be the "dopamine addiction hits" you get from multitasking, oxytocin because of public recognition from your boss, the serotonin feel-good from the sun on your face, or endocannabinoid rushes[6] at 2 a.m., when you are pushing to complete your report.

By understanding the influences that these chemicals have on your behavior, you can design your triggers–action-response–reward, or *Habits Trio*, to maximize the impact of your cravings, to form a powerful *Habits Quartet*.

Unfortunately, there is no scientifically validated way to test neurotransmitter levels [64]. The best way to understand these is to assess your symptoms,[7] and from there, optimize your neurotransmitter levels with appropriate measures (see *Mission 47: Take a Daily DOSE*).

---

[6] Recent studies have shown that it is the endocannabinoid system and not endorphins that handles the mood-boosting effects of positive emotions [63].

[7] For a quick reference, you can review sample symptoms at https://drknews.com/neurotransmitter-symptoms/

***

🚀 Mission 34: Understand Your Current Cravings

Take a moment to reflect on some of your current habits. Can you identify the associated cravings? Ask yourself:

- How do you feel about yourself when completing the action-response?
- What do you feel in your body?
- How do you feel from a mental perspective: are you inspired, focused, calm...?

For instance, recall the prior example where you are a mentor for your team.

Your strategic goal is to leverage leadership and team dynamics in alignment with your company's strategy. Your tactical objective is to set up a mentoring program you will monitor, for example, through the number of times you hold effective mentoring sessions with your team members.

The components of your *Habits Quartet* are:

- Trigger: flexible
- Action-response: informal 10-minute sessions over a coffee break
- Reward: Positive changes in behavior and attitudes
- *... and your craving is the pride you feel, with oxytocin coming into play, when your team members' performance improves.*

***

As the maestro or maestra, **you have familiarized yourself with the components of your *Habits Quartet*. You have understood that:**

- The **triggers you define must cue the action-responses** and function as a catalyst.

- **Triggers need to boost your cravings** to want or desire the reward or to move away from the threat associated with the action-response.
- As the **association between the trigger, the action-response, the reward, and the craving increases, your action-response will become more ingrained** until you can perform it on full autopilot.

Getting this right will allow you to execute a habit without your executive system having decided. Instead, your habits system will have taken over, and it now feels easy to carry out the habit.

Armed with this knowledge, continuing as the maestro or maestra, you will now need to write up your *Habits Score*, a clean, playable, and easy-to-read and executable "notation." This will allow your *Habits Quartet* to deliver a powerful concert, just like a large group of musicians all playing together, designed to enlighten and empower.

Remember, the four components will need to be synchronized, listening to each other during the symphony, and you will need to be fully focused when you execute your action-response.

If your *Habits Score* is not aligned with your strategic goals, if any section plays out of sync or misses a note, if the opening move is not effective, if the rise to a crescendo is incipient, you may get to perform one or two acts, but the encore will not be sufficient, and your habits will not form.

From Trio to Quartet—Creating Habits

As the scientist, you understood your brain systems and how your brain can trap your best initiatives. As the painter, you crafted your vision and strategic goals. As the maestro or maestra, you defined your tactical objectives and understood the *Quartet* you will need to conduct.

Now, continuing as the maestro or maestra, to build or change a habit, you will take an active composer-conductor role. You will set up your *Habits Quartet* and begin building your *Habits Score*, working diligently on your compositions.

At this stage, your behavior will not be under the control of your automatic and nonconscious mind.

As you learn a habit, putting in place the trigger, executing the action-response, and reaping the reward, your brain will have to work at full power, as you move from the Habits Formation stage of *conscious incompetence* to *conscious competence*.

As you start practicing with your *Habits Score*, you will incur a high computational cost to make sense of all the new information, with your neurons firing continuously from beginning to end (see Figure VIII.11).

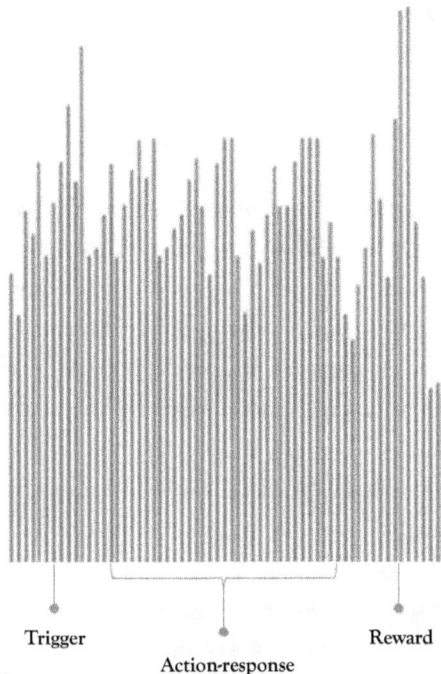

Trigger   Reward

Action-response

Figure VIII.11 Habits trio firing

This is going to be challenging work, but with repeated practice of your *Habits Score*, your well-synchronized *Habits Trio* (trigger–action-response–reward) will lead to your behavior becoming more automatic.

This will allow you to move from *conscious competence* to *unconscious competence*, with your craving becoming more spontaneous.

By understanding this build-up from *Habits Trio* to *Habits Quartet*, you can build or rebuild patterns in whichever way you choose (see Figure VIII.12).

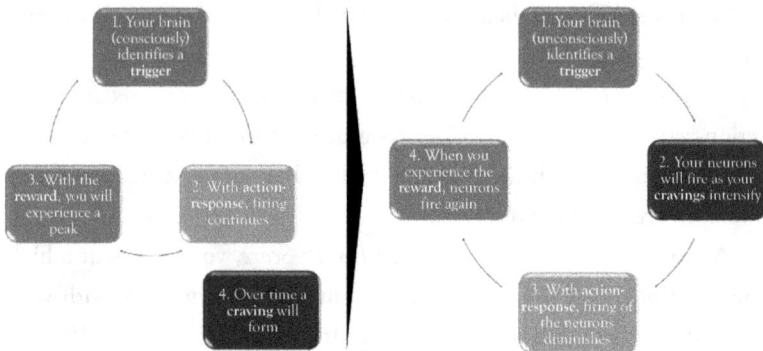

Figure VIII.12 From trio to quartet

Compose Your Habits Score

The choice you make to envision your future and design and implement your *Habits Quartet* and *Habits Score* will affect your journey in life, as many habitual moments comprise your days, weeks, months, and years.

With your *Habits Quartet* playing powerful *Habits Scores*, you will create a repertoire of great habits, leveraging behaviors and cultures by explicit decisions rather than developing these inadvertently and instinctively.

How do you go about this task? You will need to build your habits through the sequential steps shown next (see Figure VIII.13):

1. Define your action-responses.
   - Which habits do you want to create?
   - Which action-responses do you need to put in place?
2. Define your triggers.
   - Now that you've defined your action-responses, you can define and implement your arsenal of triggers.
   - Remember to carry out the ACIDS test to determine whether the triggers are adequate.
3. Define your rewards.
   - Define the rewards associated with the action-responses.
   - Review the reward categories and dimensions to ensure they fit with the action-responses.

4. Define your cravings.

- Review the objective outcomes you desire and think of the potential cravings, linking these to the rewards you have defined.

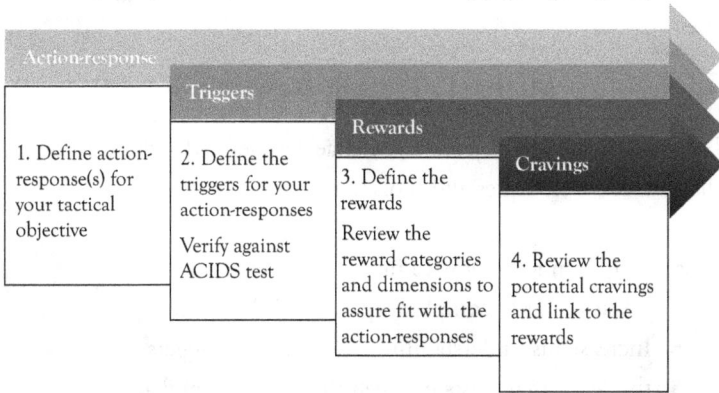

Figure VIII.13 Creating Habits Scores

With this sequence, you will create a repertoire of *Habits Scores*. You then need to practice conducting your *Habits Quartet*, occasionally rewriting parts of the *Habits Score*, as you guide your *Quartet* through your compositions.

By excelling as both a composer and a conductor, you will move from routine rehearsals to world-class performances.

***

🚀 Mission 35: Define Your Action-Responses

Based on your tactical objectives, you can now define your action-responses for the habit you wish to create. Before you move forward with your mission, review Michael's tactical objectives and action responses.

***

Michael's Tactical Objectives

- I will practice and cultivate essential skills daily to regulate my emotions.
- I will positively power all disturbing impulses in potential threat situations and keep them in check as these arise.

Michael's Action-Responses

Based on his tactical objectives, Michael has defined action-responses that include techniques and tools that will:

- Help him learn how to manage signals from the extraordinarily complex organ that is his brain.
- Increase his understanding of emotional triggers and the "gap" that exists between these triggers and action-responses.
- Help him become better equipped to react positively and with greater awareness to threat situations.

In Michael's case, the action-responses he defined were twofold:

I.   Integrated emotional regulation techniques
II. Consequential thinking

As mentioned in the section *Action-Response—Focused Tempo*, these action-responses will also help you augment your focused attention density. Let's look at these.

Action-Response I—Integrated Emotional Regulation Techniques

The integrated emotional regulation techniques, as the name implies, include diverse solutions—**alternating breathing techniques/direct experience/binaural beats—that you can practice together**

or separately, to consciously control your brain, rapidly induce calmness when under stress or anxiety, and improve your focused attention density.

An overview of these action-responses is shown next, with further details provided in Appendix I.

Alternating Breathing Techniques

There are many types of breathwork techniques, with unique purposes and different effects associated with each technique.

Michael rotates these techniques over the course of the week or uses a specific technique for certain situations. He alternates between gentler sequences like alternate nostril breathing or extended exhale breathing, and the physiological sigh or box breathing.

Direct Experience

Direct experience or moment-to-moment experience is a scientific term used to describe mental training techniques with ancient origins that allow you to experience information with your senses in real time.[8]

This technique falls within "a family of self-regulation practices that aim to bring mental processes under voluntary control through focusing attention and awareness" [65].

This will allow you to identify subtle triggers and cravings more accurately, improve your cognitive control [66, 67], and become less imprisoned by your habits.

Binaural Beats

Binaural beats are an emerging, semiexperimental form of sound wave therapy. It is an auditory illusion obtained when two sounds

---

[8] Also commonly known as meditation.

of slightly different frequencies are played through headphones in separate ears simultaneously [68].

The human brain perceives the creation of a new, third tone. This resulting frequency is equivalent to the difference between the two tones being played.

A frequency with a stable periodicity will evoke a cortical response, and the brain will eventually synchronize its dominant brainwave frequency with that of the external stimulus.

Proponents of this therapy point to benefits such as reduced stress and anxiety and increased focus.

Action-Response II—Consequential Thinking

Consequential thinking is a technique where the likely outcomes of behaviors before enactment are considered by the individual [69].

With this technique, both emotional intelligence and critical analysis are important for assessing the pros and cons of courses of action.

Creating a Habits Pyramid

As you define and execute your action-responses and create habits, **you can consolidate your action-responses further and increase the scope of your habits by creating a *habits pyramid*.**

Creating a *habits pyramid* is a tactic that leverages one small habit to create "bigger" habits,[9] by adding a habit to an existing one. Compare this to placing blocks one on top of another, building up from a square or triangular base and sloping sides, that meet in a point at the top, forming a solid pyramid.

---

[9] This concept was called "Habit Stacking" by author S.J. Scott in his 2014 book *Habit Stacking: 97 Small Life Changes That Take Five Minutes or Less*, "Anchoring" by B.J. Fogg in his Tiny Habits Method (see www.tinyhabits.com/), and "Habit Stacking" by James Clear in his book *Atomic Habits*. Generically, the objective of this approach is to use current habits as triggers to create or change habits.

In certain situations, you can create habits by using an existing habit as a trigger. These current habit triggers may occur at specific or random times during the working day and may occur before, during, or after the habit you wish to create or change. This tactic is illustrated next:

Use current habit as a Trigger → New Habit

The *habits pyramid* tactic works well because you link your new habit to an action you already carry out. A simplified example is illustrated in Table VIII.4.

Table VIII.4 Habits pyramid

Current habit trigger	10-minute kaizen meeting
→ New habit	Note-taker takes notes of actions on his laptop
→ New habit	End of the meeting: the note-taker will read out actions to guarantee alignment and approval
→ New habit	After approval, the note-taker will e-mail all participants with the link to the action-item database

As seen earlier, the fundamental elements for ensuring that this tactic works well are:

- **Coupling a new habit to an existing event.** Do this within your current schedule, to help you easily move from a current process to a new reality. In effect, you are taking a well-formed neural pathway and adding to this pathway.
- The **new habit complements a current habit**, promoting resonance. This leads to lower consumption of brain energy, as you are not trying to force your brain to build a completely new pathway.
- The **new habit should not take a long time to complete.** This will ease the process of habit creation. In the example earlier, the new habit would take roughly five minutes.
- The **new habit intensifies current or creates new rewards and cravings**. From the example earlier, the reward linked

to the trigger and action-responses is a more efficient team, giving you and your team a sense of pride and a potential release of oxytocin and dopamine.

✳✳✳

🚀 Mission 36: Create a Habits Pyramid

For this mission, first think of an existing habit. Now, to create a *Habits Pyramid*, think of action-responses that you can couple onto the existing habit. Use your workbook to complete this mission.

✳✳✳

Defining Your Triggers

Now that you've defined your action-responses and created a Habits Pyramid, you are ready to move to the second step. Before defining your triggers, let's look at Michael's example.

Michael's Triggers

Recall Michael's tactical objectives of "responding functionally to conflict situations."

From Michael's experience, he knows that negative emotions tend to trigger bad habits. For example, when diminished or addressed by a colleague in a rude tone, Michael acts instinctively, responding in a similar manner.

Michael knows that these emotions in the workplace are common triggers for dysfunctional behavior and that he will need to acquire the tools and techniques to better manage and regulate his emotions.

Given his action-responses, Michael has opted for two types of triggers (see Table VIII.5).

Table VIII.5 Michael's triggers

Action-response	Trigger	Description
I. Integrated emotional regulation techniques	Time-based trigger, more static, structured, and oriented to the long term	Alternating breathing techniques, every weekday, from 8:50 to 9:00, triggered by a calendar alert
	Preceding event trigger, more dynamic, flexible, and focused in the short term	Physiological sigh or box breathing, in response to (perceived) threat situations
II. Consequential thinking	Time-based trigger, more static, structured, and oriented to the long term	Each Monday, from 9:00 to 9:15, triggered by calendar alert

***

🚀 Mission 37: Define Your Triggers

Think of the habits and action-responses that you want to create or change. Make a list of the potential triggers (the list shouldn't be long), by answering the following questions:

- What are your potential triggers for the action-response?
- Which category is it related to (see Table VIII.6)?
- Can you select multiple, flexible triggers for the habit you want to create?
- What would be the best trigger for your habit?
- Does the trigger lead you to execute an action-response? When (you feel that) the triggers selected do not lead to your action-response, you may need to choose a different trigger or add further triggers for this action.

Table VIII.6 Trigger categories

Category
A preceding or subsequent event
Time-based
Location/object
People
Emotion

***

In the following section, you will look at how you can set up contingency plans for potential obstacles, giving you added flexibility to execute your action-response.

Creating Instant Habits

You've just initiated the action-response set in motion by the trigger you have defined. Your environment is working for you, and you are focused as you execute your action-response.

Just then, your phone rings; it is your CEO. You answer the phone and say. "Hello John, I'm in the middle of an important activity. If this call is not urgent, can I get back to you in 30 minutes?" You've just activated your "implementation intention" or "instant habit"[10] for your action-response [70].

Implementation intentions are if–then or when–then plans that guide your behavior, by defining alternative responses that can overrule habitual ones, as illustrated in Table VIII.7.

Table VIII.7 Instant habits

If … Obstacle occurs before or during habit
Then … Instant Habit

The flexibility of being able to choose your behavior when faced with obstacles during your action-response increases if you have strong and alternative instant habits.

In the example earlier, "**If** my phone rings during my action-response, **then** I will check if it is urgent, before suggesting I call back in 30 minutes."

With this if–then or when–then planning, you can define a desired in-the-moment response to potential obstacles. You will not opt for your habitual response or bank on your decision making when your willpower could be at its lowest.

From a brain perspective, locking your decision in relation to a certain event (the phone rings) with an automatic behavior (replying "Is your call urgent?") establishes a powerful basis for instant habits.

---

[10] Term used by Peter Gollwitzer to describe implementation intentions.

Add to this "that if–then planners are about 300% more likely than others to reach their goals [71]" and you have another powerful tool to add to your arsenal!

Look at Michael's instant habits before your next mission.

Michael's Instant Habits

- When in a conflict situation, if I feel anger rising, then I will remember to breathe deeply and consider that a long-term relationship is important.
- If I get a phone call during the action-response, I will check if it is urgent. If it is not, I will schedule a call for later in the morning or afternoon.
- If a colleague asks to talk before or during the action-response, I will check if it is urgent, then I will tell him I'm happy to talk later.
- If I must attend a meeting before the action-response, then I will tell the organizer I must leave the meeting five minutes before the time scheduled for the action-response.
- I will check for important e-mails 15 to 30 minutes before my action-response, and if feasible, I will answer these before the action-response. I will not check e-mail again until the next slot for checking e-mail.
- I will ensure that I am energized before executing the action-response, so my focused attention density is fully directed.

***

🚀 Mission 38: Create Your Instant Habits

In this mission, you will carry out two exercises. In the first, you will list potential obstacles that may impede you from executing your action-response, for example:

- Demands of other people
- Technological distractions

- Multitasking
- Low energy levels

After you have drawn up a list of different obstacles, you can define your instant habits. You can complete this mission using the template provided in the workbook.

Once you have completed this mission, you can move forward to the third step, defining your rewards, the encore of your *Habits Quartet*.

***

Rewards for Your Action-Responses

When defining your rewards, you need to be sure that they are not only short-term oriented, but they contribute to your long-term benefits.

Just as with the other three steps, give yourself time and space to get this step right. As you will recall, defining a great reward increases the repeatability of your behaviors.

Michael's Rewards

In Michael's case, the different techniques and action-responses he has put in place have allowed him to achieve a state of "balanced emotions" in the long term.

This has had a profound personal impact. He is calmer under conflict situations, and his composure has had a positive collateral impact on his team leaders, a situation of which he is proud.

Although Michael understood that regulating his emotions would eventually help him, he knew that he needed to choose rewards that would also give him "immediate hits" in the short term.

His rewards are shown in Table VIII.8, and the categories and dimensions of two of his rewards are shown in Tables VIII.9 and VIII.10.

Table VIII.8 Michael's rewards

Action-response	Trigger	Description	Reward
I. Integrated emotional regulation techniques	Time-based trigger, more static, structured, focused in the medium-term outcome	Alternating breathing techniques, every weekday, from 8:50 to 9:00, triggered by a calendar alert	A good start to the day
	Preceding event trigger, more dynamic, flexible, and focused in the short term	Physiological sigh or box breathing, in response to (perceived) threat situations	Reacting calmly in conflict situations
II. Consequential thinking	Time-based trigger, more static, structured, and oriented to the medium to long term	Each Monday, from 9:00 to 9:15, triggered by calendar alert	Certainty in how he will be able to respond to potential threat situations Instant habits coming into play

Table VIII.9 Reward 1—Categories and description

Reward description			
A good start to the day			
Reward category			
Social	Psychological	Physical	Other (specify)
	X		
Dimension description			
Temporal proximity (immediate/delayed)	Immediate		
Duration (short lived/medium/long duration)	Short, increases over time		
Emotional intensity (low/medium/high)	Medium to high		
Novelty (novel/familiar)	Initially novel, will become familiar with practice		
Nature (intrinsic/extrinsic)	Intrinsic		
Tangibility (tangible/intangible)	Intangible		

Table VIII.10 Reward 2—Categories and description

Reward description			
Certainty in how he will be able to respond to potential threat situations. Instant habits coming into play.			
Reward category			
Social	Psychological	Physical	Other (specify)
X	X		
Dimension description			
Temporal proximity (immediate/delayed)	Delayed		
Duration (short lived/medium/long duration)	Medium to long		
Emotional intensity (low/medium/high)	High		
Novelty (novel/familiar)	Initially novel, will become familiar with practice		
Nature (intrinsic/extrinsic)	Intrinsic		
Tangibility (tangible/intangible)	Intangible		

To generate other short-term rewards, Michael will put in place diverse measures to monitor the positive results of his short-term performance (see *Voyage IX: Full Cycle—From Tactics to Strategy*). He will also use the technique of visualization to generate short-term virtual rewards (*see Voyage XI: Move Your Vision and Goals Closer*).

***

🚀 Mission 39: Define Your Rewards

Based on the earlier example, you can now define your rewards, categories, and dimensions, for your action-responses. Complete this mission in your workbook.

***

Understanding Cravings

In effect, it is your cravings, or more precisely your neurotransmitters, which will ultimately elevate your *Habits Quartet* to a crescendo.

Recall that your neurotransmitters are chemical messengers that neurons use to communicate through your nervous system (see *Voyage VIII: The Habits Tactical Sheet*, section *Cravings—The Rise to Crescendo: Preliminary Encore*).

When your brain is activated by a trigger, your neurotransmitters fire, locking into the potential reward.

Becoming conscious of and understanding the general functioning of your cravings facilitates building habits. To work out which cravings may be driving specific habits may initially take some time.

During this period, think of yourself as the maestro or maestra, experimenting with your *Habits Quartet*. Experiment with different rewards and think of the associated cravings or neurotransmitters you may be activating. This is an essential process in creating or redesigning habits.

Using Michael's action-response as an example, let's see how this process would work.

Imagine practicing direct experience in sync with box breathing (action-response) when you wake up (trigger).

When you wake up, measure your pulse rate. After practicing the techniques, you will feel calmer. Now immediately measure your pulse rate again and compare it with the initial measurement. Feeling calm and the decrease in your pulse rate are your rewards; these techniques have both qualitative and measurable benefits!

Think about how calm you feel. This is GABA, the calming and relaxation neurotransmitter at play. Then think about the dopamine rush you will feel, as you know that these action-responses are minimizing your stress levels and improving your focus.

Eventually, these cravings will occur naturally when you wake up, making it easier to push through on your action-response.

Michael's Habits Score

Look at Michael's *Habits Score*, including the cravings he has defined (see Table VIII.11).

Table VIII.11 *Michael's Habits Score*

Action-Response	Trigger	Reward	Craving
Alternating breathing techniques	Every weekday, 8:50 to 9:00, triggered by a calendar alert	A good start to the day	Improve global disposition (GABA/serotonin)
Physiological sigh or box breathing, in response to (perceived) threat situations	Preceding event trigger, more dynamic, flexible, and focused in the short term	Reacting calmly in conflict situations	Reduce anxiety levels (adrenaline and cortisol)
Consequential thinking	Each Monday, from 9:00 to 9:15, triggered by calendar alert	Reacting calmly in conflict situations	Reduce anxiety levels (adrenaline and cortisol)

***

🚀 Mission 40: Define Your Cravings

Based on the examples shown, define your cravings, considering your triggers, action-responses, and rewards. Complete this mission in your workbook.

***

Now that you've defined your *Habits Score*, you need to implement your score and practice. As the maestro or maestra, your role is to ensure that you expertly conduct your *Habits Quartet* to a powerful *Habits Score*.

You should carry out the following mission regularly, to determine if you are on track.

***

🚀 Mission 41: Habits Score Checkpoint

As you practice, ask yourself frequently:

- Does the trigger cue the craving?
- Do I miss notes? Am I receiving an encore at the beginning and the end of my performance?

- Is my focused attention density directed as I execute my action-response?
- As the habit develops, am I able to identify the craving when triggered?
- Before executing my action-response, am I able to identify and feel the sensations when I am activated by the trigger?

***

You are now executing your tactics and you begin to feel good as it all comes together (see Figure VIII.14). Let's recap your strategic–tactical voyages to date.

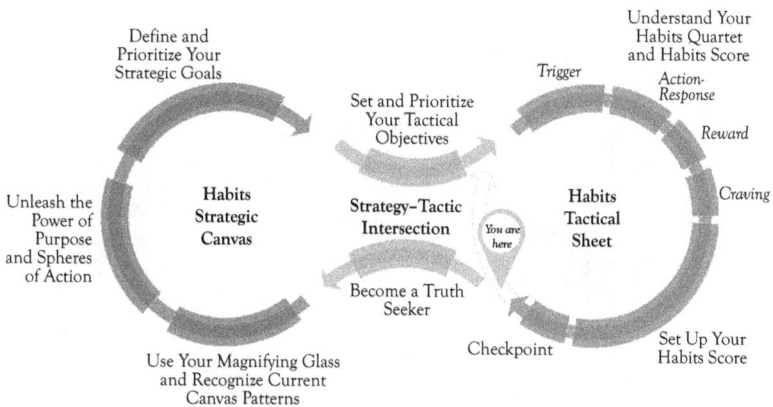

Figure VIII.14 Become a truth seeker

As the **painter**, you ran the extra mile, and you:

- **Defined your vision, SoA, and strategic goals**

As the **maestro or maestra**, you:

- **Broke down your goals** into tactical objectives
- **Understood your Habits Quartet**
- **Built up your Habit Scores**

You now ask yourself, "How do I know whether I'm all the way there? How will I know if I've crossed the finish line?"

To know this, you will have to become a *Truth Seeker* [72]. You will need to monitor your progress and your outcomes related to both your strategic goals and tactical objectives.

Ready to take on this challenge? It is now time for your final voyage as the maestro or maestra.

VOYAGE IX

Full Cycle—From Tactics to Strategy

It is wrong to suppose that if you can't measure it, you can't manage it.
—W. Edwards Deming

In your final voyage as the maestro or maestra, you have **one final ambitious objective**:

⊕ To **monitor your goals, objectives, and results**.

***

To achieve this objective, you will need to execute one mission:

🚀 Mission 42: Become a Truth Seeker

***

As you've seen, your brain is a machine that protects the status quo. Attempting to acquire new habits can send out alarms, even more so when you consider monitoring your goals, objectives, and results. This may be because your "brain's threat avoidance real estate" feels it needs to avoid potentially disappointing feedback.

Yes, monitoring the results of the execution and outcome of your *Habits Score* and associated tactical objectives can be hard work and painful, especially if you are off-track.

But the longer-term disappointment from not achieving your vision and strategic goals will be even higher. This may lead you once again into a spiral of making excuses and blaming your fluctuations in willpower, low levels of motivation, daily distractions, or lack of time.

Monitor Your Strategy and Habits

Deep down, you know that it is only by measuring that you will have proof of whether you are successfully creating habits. In effect, as stated by Stacey Barr, when it comes to performance measurement, you need to become a *Truth Seeker*.

If you want to master the science and art of creating habits, if you want to be a lifelong learner, you will need to master the science of performance monitoring and feedback.

To be successful in incorporating and consolidating performance measurement into your habit creation process, there are several fundamental aspects you need to consider.

1. **Make it safe for your brain**

   Monitoring your achievements is a catalyst that induces a performance-oriented habit creation process. Measuring your progress and outcome has to be made safe for your brain. As Stacey Barr states in relation to performance measurement, "…we have to make it psychologically safe…."

   This means understanding that:
   - Performance monitoring will allow you to decide based on performance information rather than your emotional state.
   - Performance monitoring is about learning from the results of your measures and understanding that setbacks are part of the process of achieving your objectives. It is not about blaming yourself or others, it is about learning from errors.
   - You may feel anxious about failure, but subconsciously feel even more anxious about not influencing your process as you build or change habits, leading to intense away states.
   - Curiosity about your results is essential to understand what happens as you create or change habits and why it happens. Use performance monitoring to learn and not to recriminate yourself. Make it safe—this is a mindset shift that moves you to a toward state and will allow you to start winning.

2. **Make it real**

   Understand that performance monitoring is part of actual work. It takes time and effort.

You will need to consider diverse factors in setting up your monitoring system, including which indicators you will use to measure your progress and outcomes of your actions; when you will monitor your habits; the frequency of monitoring; what tools you will use to monitor your actions; and how you will record this information.

3. **Use tactical and strategic measures**

Across the shorter timescales, your attention needs to be on the tactical objectives and the execution of the action-response.

Monitoring the progress of creating habits is fundamental, as it will allow you to detect where and when you are going off-track and apply corrective actions as required.

Once you have achieved these, you can monitor the targets related to your strategic objectives.

4. **Use quantitative and qualitative measures**

While quantitative measures show you if you are on or off-track, as stated by Albert Einstein, "Not all that matters can be measured" or as put by Deming, the Father of Quality, "It is wrong to suppose that if you can't measure it, you can't manage it."

You may find that some of your strategic goals are intangible and complex to measure. In these cases, you can evaluate and learn from changes based on your progression. You can, for example, use the most significant change approach [73]. This method leverages the sharing of personal accounts and stories that you are a part of and proud of. This will also lead to the buildup of your cravings.

Having said this, as you pursue your quest, if you can observe and describe whether your desired outcome is changing or not, attempt to define quantitative measures.

Based on the specific habits you want to create, you can also research measurement tools, frameworks, and measures that are available on the Internet. This will shorten your lead time in defining your specific measures.

You will also find that combining quantitative and qualitative measures will be effective to measure your progress and outcomes. Your qualitative measures will give you meaning and orientation, while your quantitative measures will give you hard data to back up your qualitative measures.

5. **Make it public**

The probability of success will be higher if you report your progress publicly or share your results with a "habit buddy," a point we will cover in more detail in *Voyage X: Taking Habits to the Next Level.*

By making it public, you can also request formal feedback of your progress and results from your bosses, peers, and other important stakeholders.

6. **Make it visible**

Set up an automated dashboard system that will nudge you to input data of process execution and outcome. One manner of doing this is aligning this system with the frequency and timeline of your triggers.

If an automated system is not workable, you can implement a manual paper system. This system should be visible and accessible to support you in monitoring your results.

These visible monitoring systems are fundamental, as they will help you identify discrepancies in your progress and outcomes and help you concentrate on goal-relevant activities.

Note that even if you cannot currently measure performance items, keep them on the dashboard until this is possible.

7. **Make it frequent**

Monitoring progress toward your objectives is a crucial process that comes into play between setting and attaining your objectives and ensuring that you execute your actions. The more often that you monitor your progress, the greater the likelihood that you will succeed (74).

***

🚀 Mission 42: Become a Truth Seeker

Considering the aspects mentioned earlier, you are now ready to define your measures and targets. Remember, focus on measures that will encompass your strategy and tactics, your progress, and your outcomes, and implement both quantitative and qualitative measures. Become a *Truth Seeker!*

To support you in this mission, you can review Michael's measures and targets given later.

Complete the template provided in the workbook.

***

Michael's Measures and Targets

First, recap his goals, objectives, and *Habits Score* (see Table IX.1).

Table IX.1 Michael's goals, objectives, and Habits Score

Strategic Goals	Tactical Objectives	
Within six months, I will fully understand my emotions and their impact on relationships	I will practice and cultivate essential skills daily to regulate my emotions	
Within six months, I will learn to manage my emotions constructively to leverage performance	I will positively power all disturbing impulses in potential threat situations and keep them in check as these arise	
Action-Response	**Trigger**	**Reward**
Alternating breathing techniques	Every weekday, from 8:50 to 9:00, triggered by a calendar alert	A good start to the day
Physiological sigh or box breathing, in response to (perceived) threat situations	Preceding event trigger	Reacting calmly in conflict situations
Consequential thinking	Each Monday, from 9:00 to 9:15, triggered by calendar alert	Certainty in how he will be able to respond to potential threat situations Instant habits coming into play

---

Considering his goals, objectives, and *Habits Score*, Michael has defined both qualitative strategic and quantitative tactical measures, process and outcome related, as shown in Table IX.2, and detailed in Appendix II.

Table IX.2 Michael's measures and targets

Action-Response	Measure	Target
Alternating breathing techniques	Process/tactical Count of number of times the action-response was executed	Quantitative/short and medium term 1 action-response/day
	Outcome/tactical BOLT (body oxygen level test) score	Quantitative/short and medium term Base: 20 seconds/target 30 seconds in three months
	Biodots	Color: Light blue to green—tranquil to attentive, after practice
	Smartwatch app, with tracking features	Pulse rate: 60 beats per minute, after practice
Physiological sigh or box breathing, in response to threat situations	Outcome/tactical BOLT score	Quantitative/short term Target 30 seconds, after practice
Consequential thinking	Process/tactical Ratio of action-response execution with success versus total events	Quantitative/short term 1 action-response/week
	Outcome/strategic Self-report emotional intelligence tools	Qualitative/long term Improve base score by one level on a semester basis

Through a daily check-in system and automated reminder, Michael is also documenting and sending his progress and results to his habit buddy.

As **you reach the end of your final voyage as the maestro or maestra**, you have:

- **Understood the significance of setting up a monitoring system.**
- **Set up a monitoring system that is psychologically safe** to your brain.
- **Are measuring the results** of your habit creation process.

PART 5

The Architect

A designer of the broad social, emotional, and physical organizational contexts at the points of choice, who will reduce or amplify decisions to facilitate the creation of habits.

As the novice, you understood you need a multifaceted approach to build habits. As the scientist, you understood the barriers to change and your potential to grow. As the painter, you painted your self-portrait and your vision, and as the maestro or maestra, you've put together a *Habits Quartet* and composed *Habits Scores*.

As it all comes together with practice, you see that this type of performance is not accidental.

However, to achieve world-class performance, you will need to set a higher standard. As you incrementally execute your strategy and tactics, you will need to cast a wider net to incorporate your physical, social, and emotional environments (see Figure 5.1).

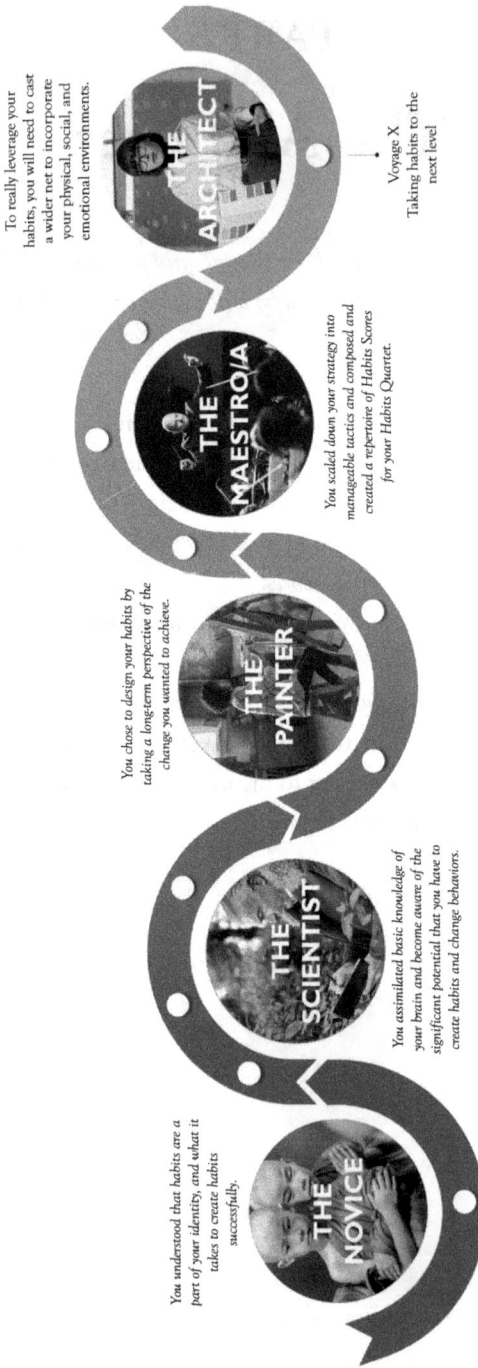

Figure 5.1 Setting up your environment

THE NOVICE

You understood that habits are a part of your identity, and what it takes to create habits successfully.

THE SCIENTIST

You assimilated basic knowledge of your brain and become aware of the significant potential that you have to create habits and change behaviors.

THE PAINTER

You chose to design your habits by taking a long-term perspective of the change you wanted to achieve.

THE MAESTRO|A

You scaled down your strategy into manageable tactics and composed and created a repertoire of Habits Scores for your Habits Quartet.

THE ARCHITECT

To really leverage your habits, you will need to cast a wider net to incorporate your physical, social, and emotional environments.

Voyage X
Taking habits to the next level

VOYAGE X

Taking Habits to the Next Level

The key to behavioral change is to pass behavioral control to the environment.

—Paul Gibbons

In your voyage as the architect, you have **one objective**.

⊕ **Design and implement stable environmental contexts** that influence you to make better choices and support reoccurring behaviors and actions.

***

To achieve this objective, you will execute five missions:

🚀 Mission 43: Design Your Environment
🚀 Mission 44: Work With a Habit Buddy
🚀 Mission 45: Create a Warp Speed Habits Multiplayer Program
🚀 Mission 46: DOSE Reflection
🚀 Mission 47: Take a Daily DOSE

***

When you attempt to build or change habits, the environments in which you perform your habits contribute significantly to whether or not you succeed.

While you may not realize it, environmental contexts influence your day-to-day choices, your professional and personal lifestyle and health, and ultimately shape your habits.

Consider the following example. A meeting you are attending starts late, as the participants arrive progressively past the starting hour. Laptops are open and people are still talking on mobiles when the meeting starts.

During the meeting, mobiles vibrate, and the ping of incoming messages distracts the participants. Coupled with a nonstructured agenda and parallel conversations, emotions flare as the more dominant voices exacerbate an already tense climate.

In this environment, it will be difficult to have a productive meeting, as options or information presented influence what gets done and even how people feel about their choices, as emotions sway in conflicting situations.

As you walk back into your office, you sigh as you see your desktop cluttered with documents you need to sign. You sit down and using your laptop, work on pending activities, switching between applications. E-mail alerts pop up constantly, and various browser windows are open.

All this distraction and clutter will undermine your willpower and your focus will be all over the place as you enter multitasking mode. Your work environment and how you relate to it will influence your choices and decision-making process.

These and similar environmental contexts will set boundaries of encouragement or dissuasion, and cueing your action-responses, with little conscious oversight [75], will shape your habits and behaviors.

Habits-Centered Environmental Design

To get your *Habits Quartet* to achieve world class performance, you will need to design and implement stable environmental contexts that influence you to make better choices and support reoccurring behaviors and actions, essential for building and changing habits.

In this voyage, you will assume the avatar of the architect and undertake five further missions. You will focus on designing three pillars—your physical, social, and emotional environmental contexts—to leverage your strategy and tactics (see Figure X.1).

Your specific purpose in these missions is to leverage sustainable habit change. To do this, you will reduce friction and increase your exposure to positive triggers and increase friction to avoid certain habits. This will promote action-responses associated with good habits.

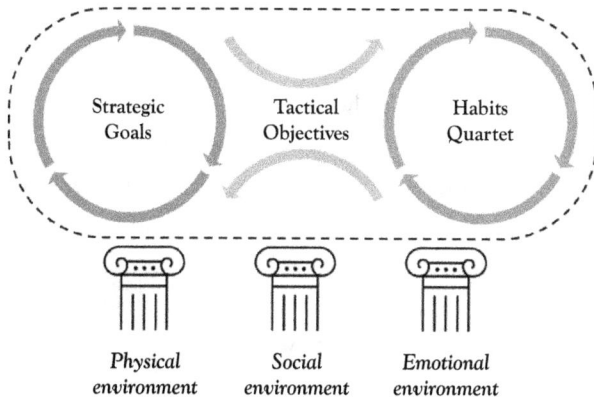

Figure X.1 Habits-centered environmental design

Design a High-Performance Physical Environment

You may think that it is only your long-term strategic goals or your short-term tactical objectives and actions that shape your ability to build or change habits, but have you ever noticed how different spaces within your organization affect the way you think, feel, and behave?

How visual cues in training rooms suggest you take part actively, how in a reception space you speak in a refrained manner and are accommodating in your behavior, and in other spaces, you speak loudly and multitask? You may have been aware of these nuances, but have you ever thought that perhaps these spaces were intentionally designed that way?

To cite just a few examples, governments are increasingly using choice architecture[1] to "nudge" thinking to improve outcomes in areas ranging from tax compliance to retirement savings, while restaurants and retailers have long employed choice architecture to boost sales.

You may think you are making your own choices, but careful planning of different variables has nudged you toward the "right" decisions. These are triggers and options in your physical environment that influence your habits and your ability to build or change habits.

---

[1] The term "choice architecture" was first coined by R. Thaler in his book *Nudge: Improving Decisions About Health, Wealth, and Happiness,* to describe how insights from behavioral economics could be used to influence choices, without changing their objective values. Thaler and coauthor C. Sunstein expanded on a concept described in the 1990 book, *The Design of Everyday Things,* by D. Norman, a cognitive scientist and design researcher.

How can you design organizational spaces to encourage certain types of behavior, such as individual work or collaboration? How can you design options at the point of choice so that these shape your actions and influence decisions throughout your working day? How can you set up spaces so that changing or creating habits also becomes associated with the entire contextual physical environment where the habit is executed?

In summary, how can you design your workplace environments to support the habits that generate performance, diversity, inclusion, and other fundamental organizational drivers?

Choice Architecture in Action

There is no such thing as a neutral environment. If you fail in executing easily triggered action-responses, remember that this may come down to poor environmental design.

As an architect, you will need to design and build "feeling into your environment" to influence what you do and how you feel about your choice.

You have at your disposal choice architecture tools[2] that will help nudge[3] you toward creating or changing habits.

Let's look at how you can leverage some of these tools in an organizational context, using the prior example of the meeting environment.

Reduce Choice Overload

You feel that you like to have choices (more is better), but too many choices will overwhelm your executive system and may lead to decision fatigue.

As an architect, you can reduce choice overload (less is better) from your decision-making process, by either structuring or limiting the alternatives of potential choices.

---

[2] Adapted from the tools described by R. Thaler and C. Sunstein in their classic book *Nudge: Improving Decisions About Health, Wealth, and Happiness.*

[3] A nudge is any aspect of the choice architecture that will alter behaviors predictably without excluding options or significantly changing their incentives.

For the meeting example, to reduce choice overload, the meeting organizer should send a clear, well-structured agenda beforehand and present it when the meeting starts.

The agenda items illustrate the sequence and points to be discussed (no more, no less), simplifying the decision-making process for the executive system.

Make Default Options Visible

A default is a preselected choice, meaning that individuals will have to take active steps to select another option. With all things equal, people will more likely choose an option that is readily available and visible in the environment.

Let's go back to our meeting room. Imagine walking to the meeting room. A sign on the meeting room door says, "Focus and Finish on Time."

As you walk into the meeting room, pay attention to the posters on the wall with the meeting rules (see Figure X.2).

At the end of the meeting, as you walk to the closed door, a sign on the door says, "Thanks for Being Productive."

OUR PRODUCTIVE MEETING RULES	
1	Our meetings have clear, simple, and objective goals.
2	Our meetings start and end on time.
3	The duration of this meeting is short. If longer meetings are needed, short breaks should be included in the agenda.
4	Participants come to the meeting prepared. Preparation for the meeting is simple.
5	The status of pending action items is reviewed and updated.
6	Side conversations will be quickly identified and discontinued or moved to another meeting.
7	Debates will be focused on the purpose of the meeting, on ideas and not people.
8	The meeting will be positive, energetic, and motivating.
9	All elements will participate actively. The meeting coordinator will ensure that all voices are heard.
10	Decisions and actions are communicated and published at the end of the meeting.

Figure X.2 Poster with meeting rules

These visible options have subconsciously pushed you to focus, keep to the agenda, and finish on time.

Choice Over Time

Some outcomes of the choices you make will only transpire in the future. For example, constantly surpassing the stipulated time for the meeting will result in less productive time for other activities and will lead to an increase in adrenaline and cortisol stress levels, as pressure mounts.

The choice architect can manipulate this choice over time effect, for example, by drawing attention to the future outcomes of not starting on time or finishing late, evoking specific actions and shaping choices.

For the meeting example, a timer on the screen, showing the time left to the end of the meeting, may nudge individuals into keeping on track, avoiding side conversations and reducing procrastination.

In the scenario presented, your default option would be to arrive five minutes before the meeting, follow the structured agenda to reduce choice overload, opt to be a productive participant, and collaborate to finish on time.

You would walk out of the meeting room feeling satisfied, confident, and with higher levels of perceived responsibility and self-efficacy.

Designing Your Environment

When designing your environment, consider the following aspects:

- **Understand where you want to build your habit as you transition between different activities and spaces throughout the workday**.
  Is it in a specific location or do the locations vary? Does the space where the action-response takes place encourage, support, and facilitate the creation of the desired habit?
  Can you redesign locations that fall within the paths of your daily routines where you will execute your action-response?
- **Consider even small and insignificant details**, as these can have a major impact on your behavior.

- **Recall how your brain works**. Although highly intelligent, your executive system is error-prone, lazy, and energy-conserving. This system prefers simplicity over complexity, avoids inconvenient situations, and filters out aspects it does not consider relevant.
- You will need to **design information or options into your environment to either build cognitive resonance or cognitive dissonance** to increase or decrease your chances to carry out specific behaviors.

***

🚀 Mission 43: Design Your Environment

For this mission, consider locations that fall within the paths of your daily routines and design solutions for the elements of choice overload, default options, and time.

Before executing this mission, look at a simple example of how Michael primed his environment to facilitate building habits.

***

Michael's Environmental Design

In Michael's case, when deciding where to practice his habit, he chose his office, a place that is already along the path of his daily routine.

Michael opted to schedule his daily action-responses early in the morning—he knows that the probability of feeling energized is higher and interruptions are lower.

For this effect, he has primed his environment for future use, by putting in place a five-minute clean desk policy that he actions at the end of every day. In this manner, by eliminating temptations that could derail him in the morning, he has altered his workspace to increase exposure to positive triggers and reduce exposure to negative ones.

The Power of Positive Accountability

Habit Buddy

When you have to deal with constant and unique pressures, coming together in a peer group and being able to share stories, resources, and experiences in a trusting and confidential environment are fundamental to creating and changing habits.

It is critical to get explicit support from people that form a part of your life. Incorporating accountability into your process is a powerful manner to support you in creating and maintaining habits.

An accountability technique you can set up is to work with a habit buddy that can be a friend, a co-worker, or your partner. Much like a mentor, a habit buddy should be a person whom you trust, as you will share your quest, voyages, and missions with them.

When setting up this relationship, consider the following steps:

1. Share and explain your Habits Strategic Canvas and Tactical Sheet.
   - Your vision, strategic goals, and SoA. Communicate to your buddy what you intend to do and why this habit matters to you.
   - Your tactical objectives, including the action plan that you have defined for a specific period.
   - The details of your *Habits Score*.
2. Define the roles of the parties and expectations.
   - The key is to focus on the process and the behavior, not the success or failure.
   - Work together to monitor progress; provide motivation, encouragement, and support in more challenging moments.
3. Set up a plan.
   - Define how each person will monitor the progress of the process and outcome, to know if you are succeeding.
   - Define a specific location and frequency to review your progress. Accountability is about meeting each other once a week, a daily text check-in, or a virtual meeting to review progress.

You can opt not to work with a habit buddy, but the power of sharing your quest with a habit buddy will always be more powerful.

A recent study, for example, found that participants enrolled in a 15-week online weight-loss program, working with buddies, lost more weight and inches in their waists than those who took the course without buddy support [76].

***

🚀 Mission 44: Work With a Habit Buddy

Set up a relationship with a habit buddy (or a mentor) using the steps shown in the prior section *Habit Buddy* and the template in the workbook.

***

Set Up a Multiplayer Habits Program

Thousands of social interactions play out each day, as we adhere to social cues, rituals, nuances in languages, and nonverbal communication.

In this world, we often gravitate to like-minded peers, where our mirror neurons prime us to copy the emotions and behaviors of significant others [77].

From a brain-based perspective, this bonding mechanism in social interactions is extremely rewarding, creating a rush of oxytocin and elevating our sense of belonging and self-esteem.

It is this social mimicry that reinforces thinking, behaviors, and values, leading to shared group habits becoming cultural ritualism across companies.

It intuitively feels easier to interact as people readily understand one another and collaboration seems to flow smoothly.

While this sense of progress feels comfortable, you need to take on board that it is not necessarily good for performance, and it is these shared group behaviors that also make it difficult to shift habits in teams and business environments.

Collaborating with people from other groups, although potentially giving rise to friction and counterproductive feelings, will ultimately produce better results [78].

To maximize your chances of success, to get your team and teams across the organization to leverage habit creation and behavior change, consider making *Warp Speed Habits* a multiplayer initiative. Challenge yourself to set up a habits community by recruiting habit buddies across the organization.

Setting up a habit community will allow you to share rituals that form around a consolidated methodological approach. This will allow all to embrace the philosophy that most individuals have the strength to create habits and change behavior.

By engaging with your co-workers and peers in respectful alliances, you will ultimately transform peer influence into a positive force.

***

🚀 Mission 45: Create a Warp Speed Habits Multiplayer Program

Recruit members from across your organization and set up a multiplayer program, using the steps provided for the habit buddy as guidelines for the participants.

***

A Daily DOSE to Take On ANTs[4]

Your risk analysis system has shown you that your brain's real estate is wired toward the negative, constantly searching for potential threats, scientists say somewhere near 60 to 70 percent of spontaneously occurring thoughts [79]. This is a sharp contrast to the expectations of 60 to 75 percent of positive thoughts [80].

---

[4] The term ANTs—automatic negative thoughts—was coined by Aaron Beck, considered to be the founder of cognitive therapy, and popularized by Daniel Amen in his bestselling book *Change Your Brain, Change Your Body.*

With the average human processing more than 6,000 thoughts per day [81], that's approximately 4,000 automatic negative thoughts (ANTs) per day.

When thousands of ANTs dominate your thinking, the probability of building solid neural pathways as you attempt to create habits will be much lower.

Once again, this may seem that your brain has upped the odds against you, but you need to realize that many of these thoughts are just reflections of your emotions.

You will recall from *Mission 26: The Emotional Trigger* that emotions are just stimuli that generate automatic responses to help you avoid harm.

This knowledge—why your emotions exist in the first place and that you are wired for negativity—will initially help relieve you of this load, but you need to tackle this stacked deck differently.

You can balance the odds by "taking" a daily DOSE of the neurotransmitters shown in Figure X.3.

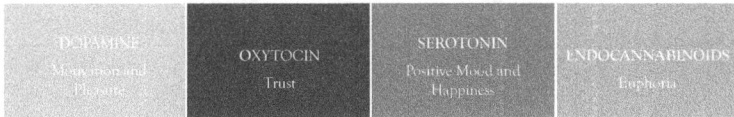

| DOPAMINE | OXYTOCIN | SEROTONIN | ENDOCANNABINOIDS |
| Motivation and Pleasure | Trust | Positive Mood and Happiness | Euphoria |

Figure X.3 A daily DOSE

Note that the biological functions of these neurotransmitters are far more complex and multifaceted than the brief descriptions included in Figure X.3 and Table X.1, although these give you a general feel for these neurotransmitters.

Table X.1 Neurotransmitter functions

Neurotransmitter	Released when	Main manifestations when balanced
Dopamine	A reward is near	Pursuit of pleasure. Repetition of goal-directed behavior, effort, and attention
Oxytocin	Touch, social alliances	Bonding. Trust. Stronger relationships with people. Positive social interactions
Serotonin	Respect, recognition, status, security	Stability. Calmness. Emotional well-being. Good sleep cycle. Increase in positive emotional processing over time
Endocannabinoids	Surpass your capacity for pain, fear, stress	Masks/ignores pain with euphoria Temporary pain reduction

Now that you have a basic understanding of the daily DOSE you will need to take, you can embark on your following two missions.

***

🚀 Mission 46: DOSE Reflection

In the following exercise, try to recall specific emotional moments in your past (see Table X.2). Reflect upon what you felt or are feeling as you remember those moments. These feelings are your neurotransmitters at work.

Table X.2 DOSE at work

Dopamine	Recall when you achieved an objective at work or received an unexpected reward. What do you feel?
Oxytocin	Notice the good feeling when someone stands up for you or you support someone, or perhaps the touch or physical closeness of someone you trust
Serotonin	Notice the feeling when you felt respected or when you enjoyed a competitive edge or when you woke up feeling refreshed
Endocannabinoids	Reimagine this neurotransmitter at work when you hurt yourself but didn't notice for a few minutes, or you felt good after physical exertion, or even after a heartfelt cry

***

🚀 Mission 47: Take a Daily DOSE

For your next mission, based on the descriptions earlier, research, define, and plan activities you can carry out to increase your daily DOSE.

You can find sample activities to leverage your daily DOSE in Appendix III.

***

In your voyage as the architect, you achieved the following results:

- **You understood that you need to build "feeling" into your physical environment** and have begun to implement solutions that support habit creation.

- You have **recognized the power of positive accountability** and the need to work with a habit buddy.
- You have understood the significance that the **emotional environment is equally as important in facilitating habit creation** and how a daily DOSE can facilitate habit creation.

PART 6

The Learner

You are yourself, as you recap your lessons and visualize what your success will look like, by moving your goals closer.

Look around. Everything that was created by a human existed as an image at some point in time in that person's mind.

Your brain is constantly visualizing future experiences using multiple senses. This happens mainly in your subconscious, so you are not aware of this process and aren't actively directing it.

Now imagine that you can consciously learn to use this process of visualization, where you employ all your senses to vividly "image" the process and outcome and enhance the performance of your action-response, create desired emotional states, and achieve your tactical objectives and strategic goals.

Many elite athletes have routinely used visualization techniques as part of training and competition [82], with significant success in the sports arena.

In your next voyage, recapping lessons learned throughout your quest, you will learn to apply this technique to augment your success in creating habits (see Figure 6.1).

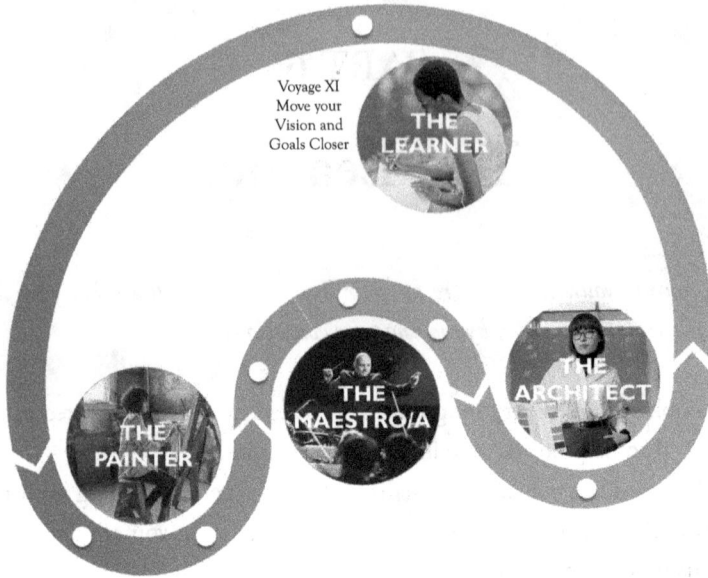

Voyage XI
Move your
Vision and
Goals Closer

THE LEARNER

THE PAINTER

THE MAESTRO/A

THE ARCHITECT

Figure 6.1 Closing the habit journey

VOYAGE XI

Move Your Vision and Goals Closer

It is not what the vision is, it is what the vision does.

—Peter Senge

In your voyage as the learner, you have **one final objective in your quest**.

⊕ You will **practice envisioning and mentally focus on executing your process and achieving your desired results**.

***

To achieve this objective, you will execute one mission:

🚀 Mission 48: The Power of Visualization

***

Neuroscience has shown that your brain can reproduce mental imagery from all the senses, including sights, sounds, tastes, smells, pressures, textures, temperatures, and movements [83], with real physiological consequences.

The mental practice of envisioning and focusing on achieving your future goals is the same to your brain as the equivalent physical experience of achieving your goals.

Your thoughts produce the same "mental instructions" as the actions in themselves. They affect similar cognitive processes in the brain, including planning, perception, attention, motor control, and memory.

By acting on the brain, envisioning alters brainwave activity and biochemistry. You will boost your confidence and self-efficacy, enhance your mood, and leverage your cognitive and physical tasks performance.

Through this important mental tool, you are training and priming your brain for actual performance and success, activating both your executive system (medial prefrontal cortex), which deals with the here and now, and your reward system (ventral striatum) where you experience reward.

By directing your subconscious as you control the images and execute the process script in your mind to achieve your goal, you are training your brain through mental rehearsals to respond as if that outcome were true in the present moment.

Moving your goals closer also allows you to bring your future *Identity System* closer, counteracting the phenomenon of "delay discounting." You will pull your longer-term rewards into your radar instead of just considering the more immediate and smaller rewards [84, 85].

To obtain the best results, process performance and the associated outcomes should be visualized in tandem.

So how can you put this multisensory experience, of envisioning all the steps from start to finish and the future outcome as if it were today, into practice?

In the following mission, you will begin to practice visualization, using the method shown in Figure XI.1.

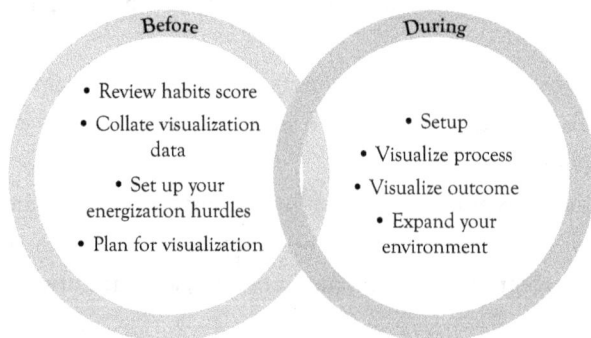

Before

- Review habits score
- Collate visualization data
- Set up your energization hurdles
- Plan for visualization

During

- Setup
- Visualize process
- Visualize outcome
- Expand your environment

Figure XI.1 Visualization

***

🚀 Mission 48: The Power of Visualization

Draw from the power of visualization by using the following method to produce more powerful results in your habit creation process.

1. Before Visualization

Review Your *Habits Score*

Review your tactical objectives and *Habits Scores.*

Collate Visualization Data

Visualization is based on imagining your *Habits Scores* being executed in full sensory detail. To do this, it will be important to find manners to expose yourself and increase your knowledge and awareness of your *Habits Scores* experience.

To create a detailed and realistic visual simulation of the four components in your mind, you can:

- Build images based on your experience.
- Talk to people who have had the experience.
- Read books on the subject matter.
- View photographs or visit the location where the action-responses will take place.

Set Up Your Energization Hurdles

Research has shown that positive thinking about your future state on its own can have an adverse effect and can lead to less effort being made [86, 87].

So, to get this exercise right, research suggests that when you envision desirable goals, you should also foresee obstacles you will face as you start your journey from your current state [88].

The effectiveness of this "reach for the stars but keep your feet on the ground"-type mentality, called mental contrasting, potentially results from the "energization" effect [87]. By considering what impedes you in achieving your goals, you will feel energized to overcome those barriers.

Plan for Visualization

A key principle to keep in mind is that you need to practice constantly. Practicing visualizing at least once a day is key. Start with five minutes and build up to 10 minutes for each session.

It is most effective just after you wake up or just before you go to sleep. In these moments, when your mind is slightly lucid, you will be able to engage your subconscious more readily and focus as you conjure up images of your process and desired outcome.

2. During Visualization

Setup

Find a place that is devoid of distractions. Sit in a comfortable chair with a straight spine when you begin the exercise.

Visualize the Process

Close your eyes, relax your body, and focus on your breathing. Take four to five slow breaths, using the box breathing method. If you become distracted or have ruminating thoughts, acknowledge them and let them go.

As you continue to relax, bring up an image of your *Habits Quartet* and *Habits Scores* coming together. Spend a few minutes imagining the details of your *Habits Quartet*. See your trigger, imagine your craving, and see yourself executing your action-response.

In the beginning, you will focus mainly on sensory images. Over time, add sounds, tastes, feelings, and even smells of the experience, and your vision will become more palpable.

Try to invoke all the senses. Where will you execute the action-response? Who else is present? What do you see, hear, smell, and feel?

Emotion will follow thought, so the more real you believe something to be, the greater the emotional impact. To enhance a simulation, keep adding detail until the process feels as real as if you were experiencing it. What are you wearing, who is speaking, what are you hearing, how do you feel?

As your visualization becomes real, you will cross the threshold that leads to action. Your positive motivational state will become enhanced, and your brain will develop neural connections that result from the visual images you have crafted.

Visualize the Outcome

As you visualize your *Habits Quartet* in action, imagine that you are achieving your goal and reward.

Imagine this mental scene as vividly as possible. Engage as many of the five senses as you can. Which emotions are you feeling when you achieve the reward? Which cravings arise? Where are you? Who are you with? What are you wearing? What do you smell and what do you hear?

The more you can relate to accomplishing the goal, the more you will believe it is attainable, and the more likely that this will lead to action.

Expand Your Environment

Enhance your vivid and convincing image by expanding your environment. Imagine your habit buddy collaborating with you; imagine taking a daily DOSE. Bring in other deliverables you have designed as an architect avatar.

Once again, imagine the sights, sounds, tastes, feelings, and even smells of the experience. Note as much detail of the scene as possible.

***

As a **result of this voyage, you will have seen that whatever your current level is, you can nurture this technique and allow it to grow.** Even if you can't project clear images, you will still gain tremendous benefits from practicing visualization.

This is a skill you need to develop. With practice, you will gain the capability to close your eyes and instantly visualize your habit scores.

Create Your Habits at Warp Speed

You've gone the full distance, taken on the role of six avatars, and executed 48 missions in 11 voyages.

You've onboarded brain-based, strategic, and tactical know-how, and you can now create or change habits at warp speed!

Wait, say what, create habits at warp speed! Is this even possible?!

A group of psychologists at the University of Zurich demonstrated successful and measurable behavior change, with 255 participants in a two-week period. The primary intervention used was two daily calls on the participant's smartphone [89].

Students and full-time working adults were assigned to two groups based on two developmental objectives. Behaviors such as exercising and improving eating habits fell within the self-discipline objective, while action-taking behavior related to openness to new experiences.

Participants received two daily calls, once in the morning, reminding them of their objective with an encouraging message, and the second in the evening, asking them three simple questions, to validate their assessment of their daily progress.

Follow-ups two weeks and six weeks later showed that the change persisted.

With further work needed to examine how sustainable these changes are, the result is inspiring. With negligible time away from the participant's daily activities, a bold target of changing behavior was achieved in a short time span of just 14 days.

Now think about this experiment. The primary interventions used to achieve this change were two daily calls (triggers) with encouraging messages (a daily DOSE) on smartphones of participants with specific (tactical) objectives.

These are only parts of the techniques and tools you've acquired during your missions as you completed your first quest (see Figure C.1). Through six avatars, you undertook 11 voyages and completed 48 missions!

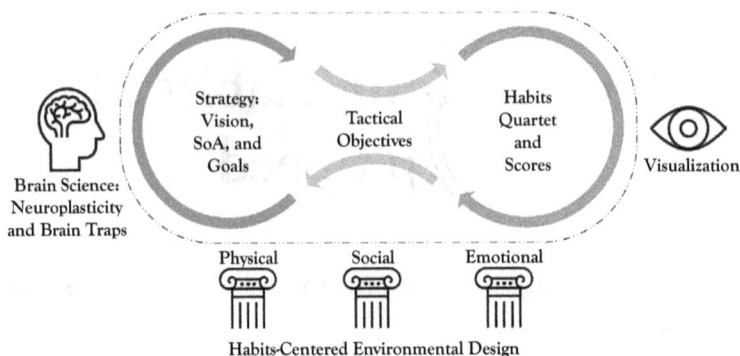

Figure C.1 A summary of your quest

As the novice, you grasped the dimensions you would need to take on board to create habits.

As the scientist, you understood the fundamentals of creating and changing habits, how to overcome mental blocks and obstacles, and the significant potential you have to learn and grow.

As the painter, you visited different realms and logged your experiences in your *Habits Strategic Canvas* and defined your purpose, SoA, and strategic goals.

As the maestro or maestra, using your *Habits Tactical Sheet*, you orchestrated your goals into tactical objectives and synchronized your *Habits Quartet* to play a powerful *Habits Scores*.

As the architect, you designed and implemented physical, social, and emotional environments to elevate your habits, and as the learner, you brought it all together and powered your habit creation skills through visualization.

You've achieved the objective of your first quest!

You have mastered a habit by internalizing the required skills within the strategic and tactical cycles. You've consolidated this experience, assumed the learning as your own and measured your success in the Strategy–Tactics Intersection.

You are now ready to return to the strategic cycle to review your strategy and start your next quest.

Paraphrasing the captain of starship USS Enterprise, "Take yourself at warp speed to your next habit!"

APPENDIXES

APPENDIX I

Michael's Action-Responses

The physiological sigh and box breathing techniques are described here.

The Physiological Sigh

This is a powerful conscious breathing technique and probably the fastest way to control your brain and rapidly induce calmness when under stress or in a state of anxiety.

The physiological sigh is a breathing pattern that is unconsciously controlled by a specific group of neurons based in the brainstem of all mammals [90].

This breathing pattern is activated spontaneously when CO_2 gets too high, and our system is triggered to breathe, for example, when we are sleeping, crying, or in situations of extreme stress.

This is a powerful calming breathing technique that you can consciously activate, to take control of your brain and nervous system and rapidly calm stress and anxiety, through two to three quick breaths in a 15-second breathing pattern (see Figure AI.1).

You can use this technique in real time to calm your brain within seconds with one to four physiological sighs when you begin to notice tension, stress, agitation, or anxiety.

Box Breathing

Box breathing is a breathwork sequence that is used to regulate the breath and was first popularized by Navy SEALs [91]. It is a technique that can be used to quickly sharpen concentration and focus and relieve stress when your body is in fight-or-flight mode. It is also a technique that

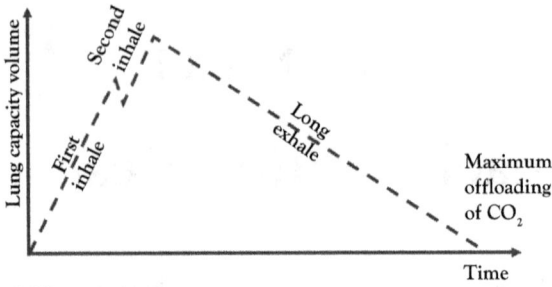

Figure AI.1 The physiological sigh

allows you to learn to control the duration of your inhale and exhale, resulting in a more powerful breathing musculature.

Box breathing gets its name from a four-sided pattern (inhale, hold, exhale, hold), shown in Figure AI.2.

According to Michael J. Stephen, MD, researcher of pulmonary medicine and author of Breath Taking, this is a technique that should be used for moments when you need a hit of quick calm, for example, before a major presentation or a conversation with a conflictual person or after a stressful experience.

To practice this breath, find a quiet environment where you can focus on your breathing. Make sure you're seated upright in a comfortable chair, close your eyes, and place your feet on the floor.

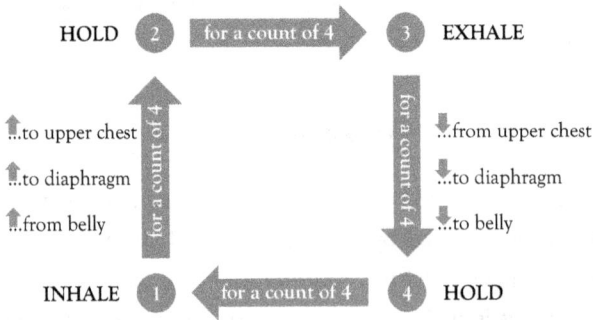

Figure AI.2 Box breathing

Initially, as you begin to practice this technique, it helps to think about the box. This technique involves four basic steps.

1. Inhale through your nose while counting to four (if this is challenging, try counting to three instead of four. Once you are used to the technique, you can choose to count to five or six).

    First feel your abdomen and then your lungs gradually fill with air.

    Studies have shown that taking slow, deep breaths activates the vagus nerve, which contains a large amount of parasympathetic (rest and digest) fibers [92].

2. Hold your breath for a count of four.

3. Exhale out of your nose for a count of four. Exhale at the same rate that you inhaled. Feel your lungs first and then your abdomen gradually become empty of air.

4. Hold your breath for a count of four.

    Holding your breath is an intense part of this breath sequence, and it may feel unnatural at first. Start slowly at first.

    During the exercise, it may be helpful to place one hand on the lower stomach and another on the chest for tactile feedback as you breathe.

    Continue for one minute or more. You can start by repeating this sequence four times. This will bring you to approximately one minute of controlled breath.

    Over time, work your way up to longer 10-to-20-minute sessions, but stop when you feel lightheaded.

Direct Experience

By becoming aware of your unconscious processes, you will handle information in real time with greater accuracy. For example, when you are worrying about an upcoming stressful presentation, it will help to take a deep breath and focus on the present moment, putting aside the future and the past.

The key to direct experience is to practice focusing your attention onto a direct sense. To support you in this activity, you can use a breathing technique to calm you down, as you focus on the sense.

Remember though that direct experience is not about sitting still in a quiet environment and feeling your breath. It is also about processing information about events as they occur and using all your senses to obtain accurate information about these events.

Over time, you will better manage your thought process and emotions. You will become more flexible in your responses, regulating what you say and do, and become less imprisoned by your habits and your *Identity System*.

Binaural Beats

To produce a binaural beat, the two tones must both have frequencies below 1,500 Hz with a difference of no greater than 40 Hz.

A person hearing a tone of 315 Hz in one ear and 329 Hz in the other will be hearing a binaural beat with a frequency of 14 Hz.

This binaural beat, with a frequency between 13 and 16 Hz, for example, is more likely to align with beta brain waves, promoting alertness.

The effect of the beat will depend on the resulting frequency and associated brain wave.

- Beta waves (13 to 16 Hz) occur when we are awake and alert.
- Alpha waves (8 to 12 Hz) happen when we are relaxed with eyes closed, as in meditation.
- Theta waves (4 to 7 Hz) are common in the lighter stages of sleep or the transition from waking to sleeping.
- Delta waves (0.5 to 4 Hz) signify a state of deep sleep.

APPENDIX II

A Description of Michael's Measures

The Bolt Score

This score is a measure of functional breathing from a biochemical standpoint, determining your ability to tolerate rising carbon dioxide levels. You can determine your bolt score [93] as shown in Figure AII.1.

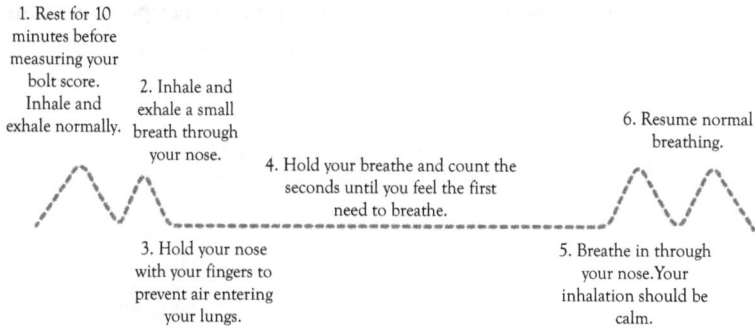

Figure AII.1 Bolt score

1. Rest for 10 minutes before measuring your bolt score. Inhale and exhale normally.

2. Inhale and exhale a small breath through your nose.

3. Hold your nose with your fingers to prevent air entering your lungs.

4. Hold your breathe and count the seconds until you feel the first need to breathe.

5. Breathe in through your nose. Your inhalation should be calm.

6. Resume normal breathing.

When you hold your breath, you have no O_2 entering your lungs and no CO_2 leaving your lungs. O_2 levels drop, and CO_2 levels rise. How quickly you feel the urge to breathe reflects your body's efficiency at extracting and using O_2 to produce energy. Compare the result with the scale in Table AII.1 to determine your target.

Table AII.1 Bolt scale

Bolt >10	Excessive breathing will eliminate more carbon dioxide than the amount that is produced through exercise. This leads to a net loss of CO_2, reduced oxygen delivery, and constriction of blood vessels and airways
Bolt >20	Room for improvement
Bolt >30	A reasonable match between the production of CO_2 from increased muscle movement and the elimination of it by breathing
Bolt >40	Optimal. Strongly correlates with high energy levels

If you take your bolt score from 10 to 25 to 40 seconds and above, you will see a significant improvement in your calmness and energy levels.

Biodots

Biodots are scientifically calibrated small dots that stick to your hand and reflect your body temperature as a spectrum of colors.

Biodots change colors as your skin temperature changes, providing real-time data on your stress level and how it reflects in your physical body.

Self-Report Emotional Intelligence Tools

Michael has opted to combine different self-report emotional intelligence tools and frameworks to measure the self-awareness perspective of his emotional intelligence. These can be downloaded from the Internet.

APPENDIX III

Daily DOSE Activities

Dopamine—motivation and pleasure

- Define difficult but achievable challenges.
- Divide large goals into small objectives.
- Create two to three goals with corresponding objectives.
- Celebrate small victories—great feats come from small steps.
- Really celebrate the achievement of goals and objectives.
- Create new objectives before achieving the current goal (ensure a constant pattern of experimenting dopamine).
- Continue to set a higher standard (but take care not to only focus on the future).
- Practice direct experience regularly.
- Harness your brain's reward system.

Oxytocin—trust

- Define the purpose of the team (most of us value helping others).
- Create team goals.
- Celebrate as a team.
- Publicly recognize high performance.
- Promote personal and professional growth—train extensively and delegate generously.
- Treat employees like they make a difference (and they will).
- Share information openly.
- Build relationships intentionally.
- Practice team-building games regularly.

Serotonin—positive mood and happiness

- Rest and sleep well.
- Increase heart rate through exercise (take a brisk walk after lunch; take five-minute breaks every hour and carry out stretching exercises at your desk).
- Ensure a balanced diet every day by opting for foods rich in proteins (turkey, salmon, etc.) and probiotics (yogurt, etc.). These contain tryptophan, an amino acid that is converted to serotonin in the brain.
- When possible, get daily exposure to the sun.

Endocannabinoids—euphoria

- Vary your exercise routine. Work new muscle groups— moderate exertion can stimulate endocannabinoids.
- Eat foods like dark chocolate, which release endocannabinoids.
- Laughing releases endocannabinoids (practice team-building games with fun objectives).

References

1. Herzberg, F. 2003. "One More Time: How Do You Motivate Employees?" *Harvard Business Review*. https://hbr.org/2003/01/one-more-time-how-do-you-motivate-employees (accessed October 05, 2021).
2. Dweck, C. 2007. *Mindset: The New Psychology of Success*. New York, NY: The Random House Publishing Group.
3. Neal, D.T., W. Wood, and J.M. Quinn. 2006. "Habits—A Repeat Performance." *Current Directions in Psychological Science* 15, no. 4, pp. 198–202.
4. James, W. 1890. *Habit*. New York, NY: Henry Holt and Company.
5. Gardner, B. 2015. "A Review and Analysis of the Use of 'Habit' in Understanding, Predicting and Influencing Health-Related Behavior." *Health Psychology Review* 9, no. 3, pp. 277–295.
6. Wood, W. and D. Rünger. 2016. "Psychology of Habit." *Annu Rev Psychol* 67, pp. 289–314.
7. Wood, W., J.M. Quinn, M. Jeffrey, and D.A. Kashy. 2002. "Habits in Everyday Life: Thought, Emotion, and Action." *J Pers Soc Psychol* 83, no. 6, pp. 1281–1297.
8. Society for Personality and Social Psychology. 2014 "How We Form Habits, Change Existing Ones." *ScienceDaily*. www.sciencedaily.com/releases/2014/08/140808111931.htm (accessed October 18, 2021).
9. Kornhuber, H.H. and L. Deecke. 2016. "Brain Potential Changes in Voluntary and Passive Movements in Humans: Readiness Potential and Reafferent Potentials." *Pflugers Arch* 468, no. 7, pp. 1115–1124.
10. Libet, B. 1985. "Unconscious Cerebral Initiative and the Role of Conscious Will in Voluntary Action." *Behavioral and Brain Sciences* 8, pp. 529–539.
11. Soon, C.S., M. Brass, H.J. Heinze, and J.D. Haynes. 2008. "Unconscious Determinants of Free Decisions in the Human Brain." *Nat Neurosci* 11, no.5, pp. 543–545.

12. Lally, P.C., C.H.M. van Jaarsveld, H.W.W. Potts, and J. Wardle. 2010. "How Are Habits Formed: Modelling Habit Formation in the Real World." *Eur. J. Soc. Psychol* 40, pp. 998–1009.

13. Finn, E.S., X. Shen, D. Scheinost, M.D. Rosenberg, J. Huang, M.M. Chun, X. Papademetris, and R.T. Constable. 2015. "Functional connectome fingerprinting: identifying individuals using patterns of brain connectivity." *Nat Neurosci* 18, no. 11, pp. 1664–71.

14. Purves, D.J., G. Augustine, and D. Fitzpatrick, W.C. Hall, A.-S. LaMantia, R.D. Mooney, M.L. Platt, and L.E. White. 2018. *Neuroscience,* 6th ed. New York, NY: Oxford University Press.

15. Newman, T. 2017. "All You Need to Know About Neurons" *Medical News Today*. www.medicalnewstoday.com/articles/320289 (accessed February 16, 2022).

16. Azevedo, F.A.C., L.R. Carvalho, L.T. Grinberg, J.M. Farfel, R.E.L. Ferretti, R.E.P. Leite, W.J. Filho, R. Lent, and S. Herculano-Houzel. 2009. "Equal Numbers of Neuronal and Nonneuronal Cells Make the Human Brain an Isometrically Scaled-Up Primate Brain." *J Comp Neurol.* 513, no. 5, pp. 532–541.

17. *Smithsonian Magazine*. 2019. "Researchers Discover the Tallest Known Tree in the Amazon." *Smithsonian Magazine*. www.smithsonianmag .com/science-nature/researchers-discover-tallest-known-tree-amazon-180973227/ (accessed February 16, 2022).

18. Steege, H.T., N.C.A. Pitman, D. Sabatier, C. Baraloto, R.P. Salomão, J.E. Guevara, O.L. Phillips, et al. 2013. "Hyperdominance in the Amazonian Tree Flora." *Science* 342, no. 6156.

19. Demarin, V., S. Morović, and R. Béné. 2014. "Neuroplasticity." *Periodicum Biologorum* 116, no.2, pp. 209–211.

20. Maguire, E.A., D.G. Gadian, I.S. Johnsrude, C.D. Good, J. Ashburner, R.S. Frackowiak, and C.D. Frith. 2000. "Navigation-Related Structural Change in the Hippocampi of Taxi Drivers." *Proc Natl Acad Sci U S A*. 97, no.8, pp. 4398–4403.

21. Coro, G., G. Masetti, P. Bonhoeffer, and M. Betcher. 2019. "Distinguishing Violinists and Pianists Based on Their Brain Signals." In *Artificial Neural Networks and Machine Learning—ICANN 2019: Theoretical Neural Computation*, eds., I. Tetko, V. Kůrková, P. Karpov, and F. Theis, vol. 11727. ICANN 2019. Lecture Notes in Computer Science. Cham: Springer.

22. Gothe, N.P., J.M. Hayes, C. Temali, and J.S. Damoiseaux. 2018. "Differences in Brain Structure and Function Among Yoga Practitioners and Controls." *Front Integr Neurosci* 12, no. 26, pp. 1–9.

23. DeFelipe, J. 2011. "The Evolution of the Brain, the Human Nature of Cortical Circuits, and Intellectual Creativity." *Front Neuroanat* 5, no. 29, pp. 1–17.

24. Park, T.Y.S., J.H. Kihm, J. Woo, C. Park, W.Y. Lee, M.P. Smith, D.A.T. Harper, F. Young, A.T. Nielsen, and J. Vinther. 2018. "Brain and Eyes of Kerygmachela Reveal Protocerebral Ancestry of the Panarthropod Head." *Nat Commun* 9, no. 1019, pp. 1–7.

25. McBride, T., S.E. Arnold, and R.C. Gur. 1999. "A Comparative Volumetric Analysis of the Prefrontal Cortex in Human and Baboon MRI." *Brain Behav Evol* 54, no. 3, pp. 159–166.

26. Vohs, K.D., R.F. Baumeister, B.J. Schmeichel, J.M. Twenge, N.M. Nelson, and D.M. Tice. 2008. "Making Choices Impairs Subsequent Self-Control: A Limited-Resource Account of Decision Making, Self-Regulation, and Active Initiative." *J Pers Soc Psychol* 94, no. 5, pp. 883–898.

27. Cowan, N. 2001. "The Magical Number 4 in Short-Term Memory: a Reconsideration of Mental Storage Capacity." *Behav Brain Sci* 24, no. 1, pp. 87–114.

28. Levitin, D.J. 2014. *The Organized Mind: Thinking Straight in the Age of Information Overload*. New York, NY: Plume.

29. Arnsten, A.F. 2009. "Stress Signalling Pathways That Impair Prefrontal Cortex Structure and Function." *Nature reviews. Neuroscience* 10, no. 6, pp. 410–422.

30. Schwarz, J.M. and R. Gladding. 2011. *You Are Not Your Brain*. New York, NY: Avery, a member of Penguin Group (USA) Inc.

31. Roth, G. 2003. "The Quest to Find Consciousness." In *The Secrets of Consciousness*. Scientific American.

32. Arnsten, A.F. and B.M. Li. 2005. "Neurobiology of Executive Functions: Catecholamine Influences on Prefrontal Cortical Functions." *Biol Psychiatry* 57, no. 11, pp. 1377–1384.

33. Vijayraghavan, S., M. Wang, S.G. Birnbaum, G.V. Williams, and A.F. Arnsten. 2007. "Inverted-U Dopamine D1 Receptor Actions on Prefrontal Neurons Engaged in Working Memory." *Nat Neurosci* 10, pp. 376–384.

34. Quoidbach, J., D.T. Gilbert, and T.D. Wilson. 2013. "The End of History Illusion." *Science* 339, no. 6115, pp. 96–98.

35. Ng, B. 2018. "The Neuroscience of Growth Mindset and Intrinsic Motivation." *Brain Sci* 8, no. 2, p. 20.

36. Kamins, M.L. and C.S. Dweck. 1999. "Person Versus Process Praise and Criticism: Implications for Contingent Self-Worth and Coping." *Dev Psychol* 35, no. 3, pp. 835–847.

37. DePasque, S. and E. Tricomi. 2015. "Effects of Intrinsic Motivation on Feedback Processing During Learning." *Neuroimage* 119, pp.175–186.

38. James, W. 1912. *Talks to Teachers*. New York, NY. H. Holt and Company.

39. Eurich, T. 2018. "What Self-Awareness Really Is (and How to Cultivate It)." *Harvard Business Review*. https://hbr.org/2018/01/what-self-awareness-really-is-and-how-to-cultivate-it (accessed October 11, 2021).

40. Sala, F. 2003. "Executive Blind Spots: Discrepancies Between Self- and Other-Ratings." *Consulting Psychology Journal: Practice and Research* 55, pp. 222–229.

41. Pittman, J. 2007. "Speaking Truth to Power: The Role of the Executive." *Markkula Center for Applied Ethics*. www.scu.edu/ethics/focus-areas/business-ethics/resources/speaking-truth-to-power-the-role-of-the-executive/ (accessed March 11, 2022).

42. Eurich, T. 2018. "Working With People Who Aren't Self-Aware." *Harvard Business Review*. https://hbr.org/2018/10/working-with-people-who-arent-self-aware (accessed October 11, 2021).

43. Fleming, S.M. 2021. *Know Thyself: The Science of Self-Awareness*. New York, NY: Basic Books.

44. Kinni, T. 2021. "Leader, Know Thyself." *Strategy+Business*. www.strategy-business.com/blog/Leader-know-thyself (accessed September 13, 2022).

45. Sy, T., S. Côté, and R. Saavedra. 2005. "The Contagious Leader: Impact of the Leader's Mood on the Mood of Group Members, Group Affective Tone and Group Processes." *J Appl Psychol* 90, no. 2, pp. 295–305.

46. Rock, D. 2018. "Tell Employees What You Want Them to Strive for (in as Few Words as Possible)." *Harvard Business Review.* https://hbr.org/2018/02/tell-employees-what-you-want-them-to-strive-for-in-as-few-words-as-possible (accessed January 05, 2022).

47. Halford, G.S., N. Cowan, and G. Andrews. 2007. "Separating Cognitive Capacity From Knowledge: A New Hypothesis." *Trends Cogn Sci.* 11, no. 6, pp. 236–242.

48. Compton, R.J. 2003. "The Interface Between Emotion and Attention: A Review of Evidence From Psychology and Neuroscience." *Behav Cogn Neurosci Rev.* 2, no. 2, pp. 115–129.

49. Cole, S., E. Balcetis, and S. Zhang. 2013. "Visual Perception and Regulatory Conflict: Motivation and Physiology Influence Distance Perception." *J Exp Psychol Gen.* 142, no. 1, pp. 18–22.

50. Berkman, E.T. and M.D. Lieberman. 2010. "Approaching the Bad and Avoiding the Good: Lateral Prefrontal Cortical Asymmetry Distinguishes Between Action and Valence." *J Cogn Neurosci,* 22, no. 9, pp. 1970–1979.

51. Elliot, A.J. and K.M. Sheldon. 1997. "Avoidance Achievement Motivation: A Personal Goals Analysis." *J Pers Soc Psychol.* 73, no. 1, pp. 171–185.

52. Becker, L.J. 1978. "Joint Effect of Feedback and Goal Setting on Performance: A Field Study of Residential Energy Conservation." *J. Appl. Psychol.* 63, no. 4, pp. 428–433.

53. Locke, E.A., K.N. Shaw, L.M. Saari, and G.P. Latham. 1981. "Goal Setting and Task Performance: 1969–1980." *Psychological Bulletin* 90, no. 1, pp. 125–152.

54. Trope, Y. and N. Liberman. 2010. "Construal Level Theory of Psychological Distance." *Psychological Review* 117, no. 2, pp. 440–463.

55. Locke, E. and G. Latham. 1991. "A Theory of Goal Setting and Task Performance." *The Academy of Management Review* 16.

56. Martiros, N., A.A. Burgess, and A.M. Graybiel. 2018. "Inversely Active Striatal Projection Neurons and Interneurons Selectively Delimit Useful Behavioral Sequences." *Curr Biol.* 28, no. 4, pp. 560–573.

57. "What's the Difference Between Emotion, Feeling, Mood?" 2021. *Six Seconds*. www.6seconds.org/2022/07/15/emotion-feeling-mood/ (accessed November 19, 2021).

58. Ersner-Hershfield, H., G.E. Wimmer, and B. Knutson. 2009. "Saving for the Future Self: Neural Measures of Future Self-Continuity Predict Temporal Discounting." *Social Cognitive and Affective Neuroscience* 4, no. 1, pp. 85–92.

59. Ballard, K. and B. Knutson. 2009. "Dissociable Neural Representations of Future Reward Magnitude and Delay During Temporal Discounting." *Neuroimage* 45, no. 1, pp. 143–150.

60. Schultz, W. 2015. "Neuronal Reward and Decision Signals: From Theories to Data." *Physiol Rev.* 95, no. 3, pp. 853–951.

61. Zhao, X., Y.C. Yang, G. Han, and Q. Zhang. 2022. "The Impact of Positive Verbal Rewards on Organizational Citizenship Behavior—The Mediating Role of Psychological Ownership and Affective Commitment." *Front Psychol* 13.

62. Matyjek, M., S. Meliss, I. Dziobek, and K.A. Murayama. 2020. "A Multidimensional View on Social and Non-Social Rewards." *Front Psychiatry.* 11, no. 818, pp. 1–8.

63. Siebers, M., S.V. Biedermann, L. Bindila, B. Lutz, and J. Fuss. 2021. "Exercise-Induced Euphoria and Anxiolysis Do Not Depend on Endogenous Opioids in Humans." *Psychoneuroendocrinology* 126.

64. Kharrazian, D. 2013. *Why Isn't My Brain Working?* Carlsbad: Elephant Press LP.

65. Walsh, R. and S.L. Shapiro. 2006. "The Meeting of Meditative Disciplines and Western Psychology: A Mutually Enriching Dialogue." *American Psychologist* 61, no. 3, pp. 227–239.

66. Siegel, D.J. 2007. "Mindfulness Training and Neural Integration: Differentiation of Distinct Streams of Awareness and the Cultivation of Well-Being." *Soc Cogn Affect Neurosci.* 2, no. 4, pp. 259–263.

67. Brown, K.W. and R.M. Ryan. 2003. "The Benefits of Being Present: Mindfulness and Its Role in Psychological Well-Being." *J Pers Soc Psychol.* 84, no. 4, pp. 822–848.

68. "Binaural Beats." 2021. www.psychologytoday.com/us/basics/binaural-beats (accessed March 01, 2021).

69. Slaght, C. 2012. *Uncommon Senses: Opportunity Theorem and Consequential Thinking Theorem.* Indianapolis: Dog Ear Publishing.

70. Adriaanse, M.A., P.M. Gollwitzer, D.T. De Ridder, J.B. de Wit, and F.M. Kroese. 2011. "Breaking Habits with Implementation Intentions: A Test of Underlying Processes." *Pers Soc Psychol Bull.* 37, no. 4, pp. 502–513.

71. Grant, H. 2014. "Get Your Team to Do What It Says It's Going to Do." *Harvard Business Review.* https://hbr.org/2014/05/get-your-team-to-do-what-it-says-its-going-to-do (accessed March 01, 2020).

72. Stacey, B. 2022. "Performance Measurement Is for Truth Seekers." www.staceybarr.com/measure-up/performance-measurement-is-for-truth-seekers/ (accessed July 01, 2022).

73. Better Evaluation. 2022. www.betterevaluation.org/en/plan/approach/most_significant_change (accessed February 01, 2022).

74. Harkin, B., T.L. Webb, B.P. Chang, A. Prestwich, M. Conner, I. Kellar, Y. Benn, and P. Sheeran. 2016. "Does Monitoring Goal Progress Promote Goal Attainment? A Meta-Analysis of the Experimental Evidence." *Psychological Bulletin* 142, no. 2, pp. 198–229.

75. Neal, D.T., W. Wood, J.S. Labrecque, and P. Lally. 2012. "How Do Habits Guide Behavior? Perceived and Actual Triggers of Habits in Daily Life." *Journal of Experimental Social Psychology* 48, no. 2, pp. 492–498.

76. Dailey, R., L. Romo, S. Myer, C. Thomas, S. Aggarwal, K. Nordby, M. Johnson, and C. Dunn. 2018. "The Buddy Benefit: Increasing the Effectiveness of an Employee-Targeted Weight-Loss Program." *Journal of Health Communication* 23, no. 3, pp. 272–280.

77. Dobbs, D. 2006. "A Revealing Reflection." *Scientific American Mind* 17, no. 2, pp. 22–27.

78. Rock, D., H. Grant, and J. Grey. 2016. "Diverse Teams Feel Less Comfortable—and That's Why They Perform Better." *Harvard Business Review.* https://hbr.org/2016/09/diverse-teams-feel-less-comfortable-and-thats-why-they-perform-better (accessed November 29, 2021).

79. Ranganathan, V.K., V. Siemionow, J. Liu, V. Sahgal, and G.H. Yue. 2004. "From Mental Power to Muscle Power—Gaining Strength by Using the Mind." *Neuropsychologia* 42, no. 7, pp. 944–956.

80. R. Raghunathan. 2013. "How Negative Is Your "Mental Chatter"?" *Psychology Today.* www.psychologytoday.com/gb/blog/sapient-nature/ 201310/how-negative-is-your-mental-chatter#:~:text=Even%20 though%20people%20claim%20to%20hold%20themselves%20 in,that%20could%20be%20referred%20to%20as%20negativity%20 dominance (accessed June 29, 2022).

81. Tseng, J. and J. Poppenk. 2020. "Brain Meta-State Transitions Demarcate Thoughts Across Task Contexts Exposing the Mental Noise of Trait Neuroticism." *Nat Commun.* 11, no. 3480.

82. Clarey, C. 2014. "Olympians Use Imagery as Mental Training." *The New York Times.* www.nytimes.com/2014/02/23/sports/ olympics/olympians-use-imagery-as-mental-training.html (accessed January 22, 2022).

83. Kosslyn, S.M., G. Ganis, and W.L. Thompson. 2001. "Neural Foundations of Imagery." *Nat Rev Neurosci.* 2, no. 9, pp. 635–642.

84. Benoit, R.G., S.J. Gilbert, and P.W. Burgess. 2011. "A Neural Mechanism Mediating the Impact of Episodic Prospection on Farsighted Decisions" *J Neurosci.* 31, no. 18, pp. 6771–6779.

85. Bartels, D.M. and L.J. Rips. 2010. "Psychological Connectedness and Intertemporal Choice." *Journal of Experimental Psychology* 139, no. 1, pp. 49–69.

86. Oettingen, G. and D. Mayer. 2002. "The Motivating Function of Thinking About the Future: Expectations Versus Fantasies." *J Pers Soc Psychol.* 83, no. 5, pp. 1198–1212.

87. Oettingen, G., D. Mayer, A.S. Timur, E.J. Stephens, H. Pak, and M. Hagenah. 2009. "Mental Contrasting and Goal Commitment: the Mediating Role of Energization." *Pers Soc Psychol Bull.* 35, no. 5, pp. 608–622.

88. Oettingen, G., A.T. Sevincer, and P.M. Gollwitzer. 2018. *The Psychology of Thinking about the Future.* New York, NY: Guilford Publications.

89. Stieger, M., S. Wepfer, D. Rüegger, T. Kowatsch, B.W. Roberts, and M. Allemand. 2020. "Becoming More Conscientious or More Open to Experience? Effects of a Two-Week Smartphone-Based Intervention for Personality Change." *European Journal of Personality* 34, no. 3, pp. 345–366.

90. Li, P. and K. Yackle. 2017. "Sighing." *Current Biology* 27, no. 3, pp. 88–89.

91. Nazish, N. 2019. "How to De-Stress in 5 Minutes or Less, According to a Navy SEAL." *Forbes*. www.forbes.com/sites/nomanazish/2019/05/30/how-to-de-stress-in-5-minutes-or-less-according-to-a-navy-seal/ (accessed June 21, 2021).

92. Bordoni, B., S. Purgol, A. Bizzarri, M. Modica, and B. Morabito. 2018. "The Influence of Breathing on the Central Nervous System." *Cureus* 1, no. 10, pp. 1–8.

93. McWeeney, J. 2022. "Measure Your Bolt Score and Reduce Breathlessness During Exercise." https://oxygenadvantage.com/measure-bolt/ (accessed May 11, 2022).

About the Author

Marco Neves is an author, speaker, trainer, executive coach, and Leadership Transformation Champion, supporting and leveraging leadership and team performance across organizations, using cutting-edge science. He created and has implemented Warp Speed Habits, a science-based approach to creating habits in business environments, and BRAIN SCANS®—leading with mind and brain, a neuroscience framework to support leaders and teams better navigate the emotional, social, and (ir)rational workplace environment, in various organizations across EMEA.

Index

Note: Page numbers followed by f and t refers to figures and tables respectively. Page numbers followed by "n" refer to end notes.

ACIDS test, 123, 124
action potential, 125, 125f
action-responses, 4, 33, 114, 116, 118, 118f, 124–127, 125f, 137–140, 187–190
alternating breathing techniques, 139
Amazon rainforest, 29–30, 31f
Amen, D., 170n4
Arnsten, A., 43
attention, 126
automatic negative thoughts (ANTs), 170–171, 170n4
axon, 26, 27

Barr, S., 154
Beck, A., 170n4
behavior change, 6, 8, 9, 102, 170, 183
binaural beats, 139–140, 190
biodots, 192
Bohr, N., 51
Bolt score, 191t, 191f, 191–192
bottom–up approximations, 102
box breathing, 187–189, 188f
Buonarroti, M., 99
Burch, N., 22n1
business thinking, 12, 12f

cell body, 26
choice architecture, 163n1, 164–166
choice overload, 164–165
choice over time, 166
Clear, J., 140n9
conscious
    competence, 24, 102
    incompetence, 24, 101–103
consequential thinking, 140
Covey, S., 88n5
cravings, 4, 5, 114, 116, 130–134, 131f, 132f, 148–150

culture change, 82
Curie, M., 19

daily DOSE, 170–173, 171f, 172t, 181, 193–194
Damásio, A., 31n12
Deecke, L., 9
default option, 165–166
dendrites, 26
The Design of Everyday Things (Norman), 163n1
direct experience, 139, 189–190
dopamine, 27n3, 43n6, 45, 131, 132, 193
Drucker, P., 87–88
Duhigg, C., 4n1, 82
Durant, W., 11
Dweck, C., 52, 54

Einstein, A., 19, 155
electroencephalogram (EEG), 9–10
emotion, 117–118
emotional drivers, 90–95
emotional trigger, 118–120, 119f
endocannabinoids, 132, 132n6, 194
environmental behaviors, 14–15
environmental design, 166–169
Epictetus, 11, 11n8
euphoria, 194
event-based triggers, 120f, 120–121
executive system, 38–40

final frontier systems, 38, 39f
fixed mindset, 52–55, 53f, 55t
Fleming, S., 70
focus, 126
focused attention density, 126, 126f
4 Disciplines of Execution (Covey), 87–88, 88n5
Franklin, B., 68, 68n3

Frankl, V., 118
functional magnetic resonance
    imaging (fMRI), 10, 10n5

Galilei, G., 19
glial cells, 27n5
Global Innovation Management
    Institute (GIMI), 80n4
growth mindset, 52–55, 53f, 55t

habit buddy, 156, 168, 169–170,
    173, 181
habits
    building, 15–17
    building block of, 25–28
    daily behaviors, 5–7, 6t
    defined, 4–5
    growth mindset for, 13
    pyramid, 140–142, 141t
    score checkpoint, 150–151
    strategic canvas, 67f, 67–68
    system, 42–43
habits-centered environmental design,
    162–167, 163f
Habits Formation Matrix, 22–25, 60
    strategy and tactics, 100–104, 104f,
    105t, 105f
Habits Quartet, 5, 45, 114, 115f, 116,
    123, 124, 131–136, 136f,
    137, 146, 149, 150, 162,
    180–181, 184
Habits Score, 102, 103, 112, 134,
    135–137, 137f, 149, 150t
Habit Stacking, 140n9
Habits Trio, 135, 135f, 136f
Hebb, D., 33
Hebbian theory/Hebb's law, 33
Hebb's law, 125

identity system
    illusion, 50–52
    mindset, 52–55
implicit memory, 5, 5n2
instant habits, 144t, 144–146
integrated emotional regulation
    techniques, 138–140
inverted-U model
    of arousal, 43–44, 44f
    and stretch goals, 93–94, 94f

James, W., 57

Kahlo, F., 60, 66
Kandel, E. R., 42
Konorski, J., 34n14
Kornhuber, H. H., 9

Latham, G., 103
learning system, 43–45
Levitin, D. J., 116n1
Libet, B., 10
location/object-based triggers,
    122–123
Locke, E., 103
long-term change, 58, 58f
long-term motivation, 127

Merzenich, M., 33
Michael, 66; *See also* self-portrait and
    canvas
moment-to-moment experience, 139
monitoring progress, 154–156
multiplayer program, 170–172

Navy SEALs, 187
negative emotional drivers, 90t, 90–91
nervous system, 27
neuronal activity, 34
neurons, 29–30, 30n9
    tree-like structure of, 26, 26f
neuroplasticity, 33–34, 34n14
neuroscience, 8–9
neurotransmitters, 27n3, 114
    functions, 171, 171t
norepinephrine/noradrenaline, 40n4,
    43n6, 45
Norman, D., 163n1
*Nudge: Improving Decisions About
    Health, Wealth, and Happiness*
    (Thaler), 163n1, 164n2

objectives, prioritization, 111–112
organizational change, 88n5
The Organization of Behavior (Hebb),
    33
oxytocin, 27n3, 132, 169, 193

people triggers, 123
performance monitoring, 154

physical environment, 163–164
physical rewards, 128
physiological sigh, 187
Picasso, P., 60
positive accountability, 168–169
positive emotional drivers, 90t, 90–91
prefrontal cortex (PFC), 38
procedural memory, 24n2
psychological illusion, 52, 52f
psychological rewards, 128
psychology, 8–9

Ramón y Cajal, S., 17
readiness potential, 10
rewards, 4, 5, 45, 116, 127–130, 129t,
    146, 147t, 148t, 148–149
risk analysis system, 40–41
Roth, G., 42

science of habits, 63
Scott, S. J., 140n9
self-awareness, 68
self-portrait and canvas
    exhibition of, 78
    fairness, 75, 77
    list and description of values,
        70–72, 71t, 73f
    mentor, working with, 77–78
    positive attitude, 75, 77
    priorities, beliefs, and behaviors,
        72, 74f, 74–75
    size and depth, 78–79, 79f
    spectator perspective, 76–77
    strategic goals, 85–96, 88f, 92f,
        93f, 95f
    vision statements, 83–85
self-report emotional intelligence, 192
Senge, P., 177
serotonin, 132, 194
social rewards, 128
spheres of action (SoA), 80–82, 80n4,
    81f, 88
Stephen, M. J., 188
The Story of Civilization (Durant), 11
strategic goals, 85–96, 88f, 92f, 93f,
    95f, 157t

strategic–tactical roadmap, 63f, 63–64
strategy and tactics, 12–13, 60–63,
    61f, 63f, 100–103, 162
Sunstein, C., 163n1, 164n2
Sun Tzu, 60

tactical objectives, 106–111, 138, 157t
    challenging, 109, 110f
    and effort level, 109, 109f
    emotional relevance of, 108, 108f
    glue-like, 108, 108f
    meaningfully measurable objectives,
        110–111, 111f
    and mindset, 109, 109f
    and mindset traits, 109, 109f
    results-oriented objectives,
        110–111, 111f
    timescale, 110, 110f
Thaler, R., 163n1, 164n2
time-based triggers, 121–122
to-do list, 4, 5, 114, 114t, 117, 128
top–down approximations, 102
triggers, 4, 5, 15, 21, 28, 116–118,
    117t, 118f, 133–134, 142,
    143t, 143–144
    arsenal of, 123–126
    criteria, 123
    emotional, 118–120, 119f
    event-based, 120f, 120–121
    location/object-based, 122–123
    people, 123
    time-based, 121–122
Truth Seeker, 151f, 151–152, 154,
    156–158

unconscious
    competence, 24, 103
    incompetence, 24, 100–101

visible monitoring systems, 156
vision statements, 83–85
visualization, 178f, 178–181

Wimba tree, 29, 29n8, 30

Yerkes–Dodson law, 43n5

www.ingramcontent.com/pod-product-compliance
Lightning Source LLC
Chambersburg PA
CBHW061158220326
41599CB00025B/4524